Tailor made C2C cycle trips
www.trailbrakes.co.uk

Trailbrakes trips are available on:
The Classic C2C ❋ Coast and Castles
Hadrian's Cycleway
Way of the Roses ❋ Reivers Cycle Route
Plus our very own 'Off Road' C2C

EcoCycleAdventures

C2C

Bike Transport
Baggage Transfers
Support Vehicles
Accommodation
Organising
Full Packages

01434 600600

www.ecocycleadventures.co.uk

Cross-Channel cycling route

Mt St Michel · St Malo · Jersey · Weymouth · Poole · Cherbourg

PETIT TOUR DE MANCHE

petit tour
DE MANCHE

A 450km cross-Channel odyssey for all the family, incorporating a Tour of Jersey

WEYMOUTH 2 WEYMOUTH
VIA POOLE, CHERBOURG AND SAINT-MALO

Coast to Coast

20th Edition
By Mark Porter

Accommodation, Food and Drink
History, Route and Maps
in the
Lake District, Pennines and Scottish Borders

By: Mark Porter
Design: Hillside Creative | www.hillsidecreative.co.uk
Copyright: Baytree Press 2015 ©

Published by:
Baytree Publishing
Primrose Cottage
Wester Ulston
Jedburgh
Roxburghshire TD8 6TF

+44 (0) 7767 893790
info@cycle-guides.co.uk
www.cycle-guides.co.uk

ISBN: 978-0-9932848-0-9

Coast to Coast

CYCLE ROUTES

Accommodation, Food and Drink
History, Route and Maps over three great Sea to
Sea rides in the Lake District, Pennines and Borders

C2C | HADRIAN'S CYCLEWAY | REIVERS

by Mark Porter

20th Edition

CONTENTS

CYCLE SHOPS
Inside Back Cover

INTRODUCTION

Welcome to Coast to Coast Cycle Routes 2015/16: Last year we introduced new, much clearer mapping and also two new loops, **Wiggo's Way** and the **Weardale Alternative**.

WIGGO'S WAY, which we are delighted to say has attracted lots of riders, absorbs the old Yellow Jersey braid between Penruddock and Great Strickland, and takes you down to the shores of Ullswater, before going on to Stanhope, **Askham**, **Appleby** and **Middleton**, taking in a majestic sweep of Teesdale, much of it along the well established **Pennine Cycleway**. Whilst Wiggo's Way does not include Hartside, it does involve plenty of challenge and a fair amount of climbing, particularly on the 13-mile stretch between **Middleton** and **Stanhope**.

It was named by locals in honour of the great Sir Bradley Wiggins who, along with the whole of Team Sky, descended upon the Strickland Arms after a local stage of the Tour of Britain in 2012.

We know that you will enjoy it and look forward to feedback on the website's Your Trips section.

THE WEARDALE ALTERNATIVE was added because a) it is less arduous than the current Nenthead to Stanhope route and b) because there are far more facilities along the way, including pubs, B&Bs and cafés. It follows the A689 from **Nenthead** to **St John's Chapel**, before veering off for seven miles or so on a charming back-road via **Horsley Hall** to **Stanhope**. This helps to benefit the local communities and avoids the logjams through Rookhope, whose facilities are overstretched even on a wet day.

THE DURHAM LOOP, introduced in 2011, has proved a huge hit. Veering right immediately after Hownsgill Viaduct, it goes through the centre of Durham as well as such villages as **Lanchester**, following the old railway lines. The second section veers right immediately after **Hownsgill** Viaduct, in the heart of Co Durham, taking in the city of Durham. We believe these additions to the C2C add hugely to the C2C experience.

Much of the information in this book is also on our websites, which can be accessed via the hub: **cycle-guides.co.uk** or on **c2c-guide.co.uk**

HADRIAN'S CYCLEWAY

Since it was launched in the summer of 2006 Hadrian's Cycleway has proved a tremendous pull for cyclists. For those wishing to voyage coast to coast twice in one trip, it is an ideal way of heading east to west, to the start of the C2C, bringing you back to your point of departure on the east coast. However, in deference to the sheer numbers who choose to do it the other way round - west to east – that is the way round on the website.

The C2C, on the other hand, is designed to be tackled west to east to take advantage of the prevailing winds. Both the Sustrans map and this accommodation guide run from west to east, so Hadrian's Cycleway or the Reivers can, if you wish, be treated as a 'return' leg for those brave enough to tackle the whole circuit, as they are both ideal for an east-west crossing.

Your hosts on all three rides have been chosen for their understanding of the cyclist's needs, a warm welcome, acceptance of muddy legs, a secure place for your bike andprovision of a meal either with them or at a nearby pub.

Please try to book accommodation, meals and packed lunches in advance, and do not arrive unannounced expecting beds and meals to be available. If you have to cancel a booking, please give the proprietor as much notice as you can so that the accommodation can be re-let. Your deposit may be forfeited: this is at the discretion of the proprietor.

Suggestions for additional addresses are most welcome, together with your comments. We are particularly keen to receive reports about the efficacy of waymarking on all three routes, and comments (both positive and adverse) on our route tips and guidance.

*Please note that the information given in the guide was correct at the time of printing and was as supplied by the proprietors. No responsibility can be accepted by this independent company as to the completeness or accuracy of all entries, nor for any loss arising as a result. It is advisable to check the relevant details when booking.

FOREWORD

This is the 20th edition of Mark's Coast to Coast Guide and it is now 23 years since David Gray and I met with keen local authority officers in the deep snow at Alston to propose this route. It kick-started an extraordinary chain of events which led to the National Cycle Network building numerous other sea to sea routes, including the 'Way of the Roses' from Morecambe to Bridlington, and Devon's Ilfracombe to Plymouth crossing, along which the Gem Viaduct and Grenofen Tunnel, south of Tavistock, will open this summer.

This guide is essential reading for everyone who would like to explore the north by bicycle. The C2C route from Whitehaven and Workington to Sunderland and Newcastle was opened in 1994 and remains the country's most popular and iconic cycle route, seen as a challenge to cycle its 140 miles in one day. But for most of us it is a memorable way of crossing outstanding countryside in easy stages. The Reivers route, through the wilder Northumberland countryside, was opened a few years later and then in 2006 the Sustrans Summer Trailblazing Ride opened Hadrian's Cycle Way in the hottest weather imaginable. The Solway was like liquid gold and the sunsets mirrored Turner's pictures.

This expanded guide comes at an opportune time. Never before has there been so great a need to encourage us to holiday at home and to travel without a car. Transport accounts for a significant proportion of all climate change emissions and tourism for half of that. A week cycling across the country and even better another week back again, instead of holidaying abroad, will make the most significant contribution within your power to tackling this pressing problem. Of course when you are cycling these routes, whether it is the C2C, Hadrian's or Reivers, you are not thinking much about these wider issues but rather the effort to keep going, the reward at the end of the day and the memories which will be as vivid as any you could have had in a far flung corner of the world.

John Grimshaw, CBE
Founder of SUSTRANS

THE ROUTE

The C2C is designed to be cycled from west coast to east coast.
This is because of prevailing winds and gradients: do it this way
and, god-willing, the wind will be behind you and most of the
climbs will be short and sharp, rather than long and grinding.
East to west is for those who like unrelentingly hostile gradients
with the wind in their face. If you want to cycle east to west, a
more user-friendly route is the Reivers or Hadrian's Cycleway,
the other two routes featured in this guide.

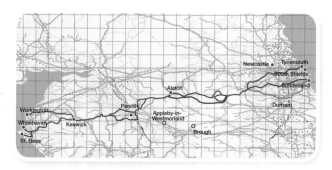

ACKNOWLEDGEMENTS

Many thanks once again to John Grimshaw CBE (Founder of
Sustrans). Thanks also to Jim Hardman for some wonderful
images along Wiggo's Way, taken last year, and to George Porter
for further research and support, both on the website and in the
book. And also to Chris Martin and his daughter Lizzy, who did
so much to help with the last edition. Thanks also to Newcastle
Gateshead Initiative, the Cumbria Tourist Board picture library,
Footprint Maps for their co-operation with the splendid Reivers
route, and thecumbriadirectory.com, whose website provided
occasional background information.

SUSTRANS stands for sustainable transport. It is a charity which
is in the process of turning many of Britain's minor byways and
pathways into a national network of cycle routes as part of a
crusade to encourage us to use the combustion engine less. It
has transformed 12,000 miles of old road, track and pathway into
the National Cycle Network, of which the C2C is a small but
important part.

GETTING THERE

TRAIN

There are three choices of start, and two choices of finish. All three possible starts, Whitehaven, Workington and St Bees are accessible by train on the local First North Western line from Carlisle. The journey follows the spectacular, dramatic coastline and takes about an hour. Remember to book your bike on in advance.

There is a cross country service to Carlisle, where you pick up the connection to the starting point of choice. In the past I regularly heard reports of the rail services being unhelpful to cyclists but I gather there has been a big change in attitude and they are now altogether more helpful – though this is at the discretion of the guard or ticket inspector. Please report back to us on your observations.

Sunderland Station
There is a ban on taking bicycles on the Tyne and Wear Metro, but they are carried by the other train operators from Sunderland station.
It's on the regional link between Newcastle and Middlesbrough/Darlington.
Cyclists are welcome on Grand Central trains from London to Sunderland, via the Durham Heritage Coast and York.

National Rail Enquiries: 08457 484950
East Coast: 03457 2252225 (sales) or
eastcoast.co.uk
Virgin Trains (West Coast): 0871 977
4222 or virgintrains.co.uk.
There are excellent services to get you
home direct from Newcastle Central
Station, (pictured)
Direct line: 0191 221 3156

AIR

Newcastle Airport is only 20 minutes from the city centre and there are regular and frequent links to many major European cities, including Amsterdam, Brussels and Paris, along with international connections to the rest of the world. Within the UK, there are also direct flights to Aberdeen, Birmingham, Gatwick, Heathrow, Wick, Dublin and Belfast.

www.newcastleairport.com

SEA

The International Ferry Terminal at Royal Quays is the north of England's main sea link with Continental Europe, with regular passenger services from Amsterdam's ferry terminal in the Netherlands. It is an ideal start point for the Reivers, Hadrian's Wall or C2C in reverse if you don't fancy getting the train across to Whitehaven, Workington or St Bees & Egremont.
DFDS Seaways
www.dfdsseaways.co.uk
0871 522 9955

TAXI

Specialist taxi services are readily available for the return journey. Some of them will organise the whole package for you.

Bike Bus, Stanley Mini Coaches, Stanley: 01207 237424
Cycle Transport North East, Newcastle: 07780 958679
EcoBike Transport, Hexham: 01434 600600
Pedal Power, Amble: 01665 713448 or 07790 596782
Yellow Jersey Cycling: 01931 712238

CAR

All three starting points are easily accessible by road.
From the south and east: take the M6 to Penrith, where you pick up the A66 through Keswick to your chosen starting point. The road goes straight into Workington, or turn onto the A595 at Bridgefoot for Whitehaven or Egremont. From the north: head to Carlisle, leaving the city on the A595. For Workington, turn onto the A596 at Thursby. Stick with the road you are on for Whitehaven or Egremont.

Most accommodation owners will allow you to leave your vehicle with them. Or you may prefer a secure long-term car park. There is one in the centre of Whitehaven.

There is a free car park one mile from the start of the C2C at one of the last mile points on the home leg of the Reivers Route, run by a Sustrans ranger. **Contact Jim Hewitson 01946 692178**. Jim runs Animal Concern Cumbria (animalconcernwest.co.uk) and invites you to make a donation towards this rescue and rehousing scheme for cats and dogs. 1 Cliff Villas, Bank Yard Rd, Parton, CA28 6NU. In Workington, there's parking at the quayside for £2.50 a day: **Contact Martin Perkins 01900 604997**.

For further information call the Tourist Information Centre: **Whitehaven: 01946 598914 Workington: 016973 31944** Back-up vehicles are kindly requested to use main roads in order to keep the C2C route as traffic-free as possible.

WAYMARKING

The route, which follows minor roads, disused railway lines, off-road tracks and specially constructed cycle paths, is waymarked with a blue direction sign complete with the letters C2C and a red number 7 – the number of the route. Rather confusingly this number changes to 71 and 14 in places, but don't be put off: it is marked C2C. Waymarks are posted at junctions and other strategic spots. Occasionally the  road surface is signed; sometimes there are just little plastic stickers posted to gates and lamp-posts. Signage is not always brilliant, but with sharp eyes and the use of a map you should not get lost. Having said that, sections at the beginning and end are notorious for the lack of signs; vandals like to trash them and souvenir hunters snaffle them.

MAPS

There is basic mapping in this guide, along with topographical maps showing profiles of such beastly climbs as Hartside. You will also need the Sustrans C2C map. If you want to, take the Ordnance Survey maps but they are bulky and the waymarking means they are unnecessary. You can easily buy any of these maps online at our webshop: www.cycle-guides.co.uk.

🚲 WHAT BIKE?

This is the single most frequently asked question on the C2C website. The route is made up of quiet lanes, traffic-free sections and full-on, off-road mountain biking terrain. The off-road tough bits, such as out of Keswick along the old Coach Road, or up to the summit of Hartside, are always optional, so there's a perfectly good alternative for a road or touring bike.

The traffic-free sections, often along old railway tracks, are nearly all on tarmac and cinder. The latter can get muddy in bad weather but there's always a road option if you wish – so long as you can read a map or have a GPS.

TOURING BIKE

Much like a road bike, except sturdier and capable of carrying panniers. They come with drop handlebars and mudguards so you don't get (quite so) covered in mud. The wheels are wider and stronger and the tyres less inclined to puncture, though you may wish to avoid the rougher sections as pushing a fully laden tourer is a pain in the back.

The touring bike will also have a wider spread of gears than a road bike, which is very handy on the hillier sections. AVOID Whinlatter off-road, Keswick Coach Road, Hartside off-road, Garrgill off-road, Rookhope grouse moor. Otherwise AOK.

ROAD BIKE

Great for roads as skinny wheels make for fast riding. But they are not so good on traffic-free, and hopeless for off-road. They are not designed to carry panniers, the double front chain ring means they are hard to take up steep inclines and they are more prone to punctures and buckled front wheels. Also, you get much muddier, as no self-respecting road bike would sport mudguards.

Having said that, you can blast across the C2C on a road bike and if time is of the essence then simply get some good all-season tyres (Continental Grand Prix 4 Seasons came out top in a recent road test, closely followed by Michelin Pro Optimum) and an OS map, and simply take road options if you don't fancy the alternative.

MOUNTAIN BIKE

Great, up to a point. Great for those stunning bits of off-road (Keswick, Rookhope etc), but are they worth the hassle? I am inclined to say no, as the fat wheels make for much harder work.

They have smaller wheels, much higher rolling resistance and are awkward to put panniers on. But if that's all you've got, then go for it: you can always swap the huge knobbly tyres for smooth ones.

HYBRID
A cross between a tourer and a mountain bike, these are ideal for the C2C, Reivers and Hadrian's Cycleway routes. However my vote would be for a tourer. Every time.

 **WHAT GEAR?**

TROUSERS
Lycra with gel pads are probably best. But you can also get baggy shorts with padding. Not everyone likes (or suits) lycra so there are options worth looking at online. You can wear ordinary shorts, but you would be well advised to get a padded liner to wear underneath, unless your posterior is seriously saddle hardy.

TOPS
It is important that your body can breathe and that the sweat you will quickly generate should be able to wick. This is why a merino wool or polyester base layer is so much better than cotton, which will leave you wet and probably cold. The weather can change pretty rapidly at any time of the year, so it's a good idea to have a medium layer – for instance, fleece. Then you will need a reflective, light-weight weather-proof outer garment for those inevitable moments when the needle plunges and the heavens open.

Remember: brightly coloured, reflective tops are best. Not all drivers are as alert as cyclists!

GLOVES
Fingerless are good in more moderate conditions. Gloves also protect the hands from chafing and offer padded protection if you fall.

HELMETS
A must, though not legally enforceable. Get one as light as possible, so you are hardly aware you are wearing it. You can spend a fortune, but you don't need to.

SHOES
SPD pedals and trainers which clip in make for the most efficient pedalling power. They make much more sense than the cleats used by road riders as you can also walk quite normally in them. If this is beyond your budget, then old-fashioned toe-clips will do.

THE ROUTE

There are three starts: Whitehaven, Workington & St. Bees.

There are two finishes: Sunderland and Tynemouth.

Whitehaven to Sunderland: 137 miles
Whitehaven to Tynemouth: 139 miles
St Bees to either end is the same.
Workington to Sunderland: 127 miles
Workington to Tynemouth: 125 miles

Whitehaven is the most popular start point but St. Bees is getting more and more votes. It's a more scenic route, also reachable by train, linking quickly with the Whitehaven route at Moor Row. It avoids a fairly dreary start from a place that can occasionally be logjammed with support vehicles and cyclists. Either of these starts takes you along the stunning old rail line up to Kirkland before a delightful lane follows the north bank of Loweswater and over Whinlatter. Arguably the most beautiful stretch of the entire route.

Workington is an altogether easier start, taking you through Cockermouth and up to Bassenthwaite Lake. It's also 10 miles shorter, so if you are trying to do the C2C over a long weekend, you can do yourself an enormous favour by starting here. But beware: the terrain between Hundith Hill Road and Wythop Beck is seriously off-road in places and you may need to carry your bike. An easy but hazardous alternative is the A66, turning right onto Wythop Mill.

Both Routes link at Braithwaite (or Thornthwaite) before Keswick.

TRAFFIC FREE SECTIONS

For those with road bikes who are determined to avoid these wonderful stretches of route, please consult Traffic Free section on: www.c2c-guide.co.uk/off-road-sections/

Whitehaven to Rowrah (10 miles)

Whinlatter – Thornthwaite (3 miles – easily avoidable)

Keswick to Threlkeld (4 miles)

Newton Rigg to Penrith (1 mile)

Rookhope to Roker Pier (45 miles)

Rookhope to Roker Pier via Stanhope (37). This misses out the tough off-road over the grouse moor.

Rookhope to Tynemouth (47 miles). Via Stanhope (43 miles).
Traffic-free total Whitehaven and Sunderland: 63 miles
Traffic-free total Whitehaven and Tynemouth: 65 miles
Traffic-free total Workington and Sunderland: 50 miles
Traffic-free total Workington and Tynemouth: 52 miles

Occasionally you get glass on the routes into Tynemouth and Sunderland, so be warned. However local councils are mindful of the amount of business the route brings in and are increasingly vigilant.

SOME FURTHER ROUTE NOTES

More and more large groups are now tackling the route. Please take special care between Kirkland and Lorton as these wonderful but narrow and windy lanes are shared by cars and horses. There have been frequent reports of large groups blocking the whole road and often cycling on the wrong side. This is dangerous as well as irritating for those who live there.

If you choose the road option coming over Whinlatter Pass and down into Braithwaite, please take good care. It's narrow and winding and there are lots of dawdling sightseers on foot and in cars.

Similarly, if you choose to go via Garrigill rather than Alston, the descent into the village is severe. If you're taking the off-road option to Nenthead, bear in mind it's very steep and rough. Not for the fainthearted and MTBs only!

WHITEHAVEN OR ST BEES → KESWICK

Whitehaven-Keswick: 31 miles (12 miles traffic-free)

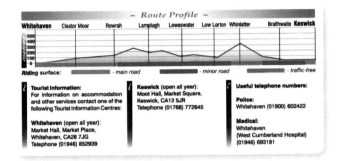

~ *Route Profile* ~

| Whitehaven | Cleator Moor | Rowrah | Lamplugh | Loweswater | Low Lorton | Whinlatter | Braithwaite | Keswick |

Riding surface: ■ - main road   ■ - minor road   ■ - traffic-free

i **Tourist Information:**
For information on accommodation and other services contact one of the following Tourist Information Centres:

Whitehaven (open all year):
Market Hall, Market Place,
Whitehaven, CA28 7JG
Telephone (01946) 852939

i **Keswick (open all year):**
Moot Hall, Market Square,
Keswick, CA12 5JR
Telephone (01768) 772645

i **Useful telephone numbers:**

Police:
Whitehaven (01900) 602422

Medical:
Whitehaven
(West Cumberland Hospital)
(01946) 693181

WHITEHAVEN

▶ DEPARTURE ROUTE

- As you leave Whitehaven harbour you will join the Whitehaven-Rowrah cycle path, which links the sea to the fells.

- First, detailed instructions for getting onto the route proper:
  Out of the harbour head right up Quay Street.

- Left past the Tourist Information Centre through Market Place and into Preston Street. Look out for signs on the left for the path behind Focus DIY.

- Onto Esk Avenue, only to rejoin the path by the school. You then cycle along Croasdale Avenue and Wasdale Avenue before linking up with the path to exit the town.

- You now follow the railway line built in the 1850s to carry limestone, coal and iron; it is now a sculpture trail interpreting the geology and industrial history of the region. You might find yourself stopping to check signage; this is routine, there are several other routes around here including the Egremont link.

ABOUT THE TOWN

Whitehaven must have more bikes per capita passing through it than anywhere else in Britain: it is both the starting point of the C2C and the finish of the Reivers route, and everyone tackling Hadrian's cycleway from beginning to end will pass through it. Once it was the west coast's main importer of tobacco and slaves. Now its slightly faded Georgian grandeur plays host to Britain's favourite cycle rides. Perhaps the most impressive feature is the redeveloped harbour front, which has undergone a £68 million facelift. There is a fine 100-berth marina, now choc-a-bloc with pleasure craft of all shapes and sizes. The town has, in short, re-acquired some of the prosperity it lost in the years after it became the world's first new town.

Not so long ago it would have been hard to imagine that early Manhattan's street grid system was based on the pattern the Lowther family laid out for Whitehaven in the late 1690s, when it became apparent that the Cumbrian settlement was destined for great things.

Shortly afterwards the streets filled with rum and sugar merchants, crews of slave ships and tobacco speculators as well as America-bound settlers waiting to set sail for a new life in the New World. The harbour was also teeming with coal transporters, which plied the Irish Sea to supply Dublin's houses and industries with black stuff hewn from under Whitehaven's seabed.

There was also shipbuilding; more than 1,000 vessels were built in the Whitehaven yards, and one of the oldest surviving iron-built ships was constructed here. After London and Bristol, this was the busiest port in England.

🔭 PLACES OF INTEREST

Tourist Information Centre (01946 598914) Market Hall, Market Place, CA28 7JG. Helpful as well as knowledgable.

The Beacon (01946 592302)
Local maritime and industrial history within the Harbour Gallery and magnificent views over the town. Done up during 2007.

Michael Moon's Bookshop & Gallery (01946 599010) 19 Lowther St.
One of the largest bookshops in Cumbria, 'vast and gloriously eccentric!'

The Rum Story (01946 592933) Lowther Street.
Exhibition celebrating the Jefferson family business, the oldest booze empire in Britain.

The Haig Mining Museum (01946 599949)
Solway Road, Kells, Whitehaven.
Memories of the last deep pit in Cumbria.

AMERICAN LINKS

Whitehaven's connections with America go deep: John Paul Jones, father of the American navy and erstwhile scourge of Britain's own, gained his sea legs as a merchant seaman from Whitehaven. Indeed, the last invasion of the English mainland, in 1778, was perpetrated by Jones upon the town. The incursion was part of the only attack on British soil by US forces; and we should not forget that George Washington's granny, Mildred Warner Gale, lived here and is buried at St Nicholas's churchyard.

The town has been impressively preserved, one suspects, because a sudden lack of prosperity after the boom years disinclined planners from bulldozing in the name of progress. This left the Lowther architectural heritage preserved, as it were, in aspic. It is worthwhile walking the streets, admiring this memorial to an earlier and prosperous age, when sea captains and merchants lived in style. There are many interesting and quirky sculptures around the harbour, a number of street mosaics featuring different aspects of the town's heritage, plus a mural in Washington Square and a plethora of shiny plaques above doorways giving clues to the past. It is one of my favourite places on the whole route and it seems a shame just to use Whitehaven as a point of departure without spending the previous night exploring. There are plenty of distractions, in the form of pubs, restaurants and venues. The following day's ride out of this port is nothing if not leisurely - a stark contrast to the undulations that are to follow. A late night is not going to spoil it.

The traditional way to start this route is by christening your bike on the slipway behind the big C2C sign by dipping the front wheel in the briny. Then you might wish to get your first route stamp at the New Espresso café in the Market Place.

🍴 WHERE TO EAT

Castle Knights Bar & Grill, Low Corkickle, CA28 7RP.
Run by: Kelly Gribbin. Rustic style, burgers, fish and chips, grills all home-cooked and locally sourced. From £7.95 to £16.95. There's a bar and a big sun trap of a beer garden, plus lock-up for bicycles. 01946 693604. castleknightsltd@gmail.com.

THE VAGABOND, 9 Marlborough Street. 01946 693671
GEORGIAN HOUSE, Church Street. 01946 696611
CASA ROMANA, Queen Street. 01946 591901
PREMIER INN. 08701977268
ZEST HARBOURSIDE. 01946 66981
THE WELLINGTON BISTRO, at the Beacon, 01946 590231

 WHERE TO DRINK

THE BRANSTY ARCH, Bransty Row, 01946 517640. Busy and well run Wetherspoons.

SUNNYHILL, Victoria Road, 01946 692291. Simple home cooked fare well executed so apt to be busy.

THE SHIPWRIGHTS ARMS, Bransty Row, 01946 692327. Small, friendly boozer near train station.

ROYAL OAK, 3 King Street. 01946 66474. One of the town's oldest pubs and known by locals as the bat cave. A small frontage hides a deceptively large interior.

THE CANDLESTICK, 22 Tangier Street. 08721 077077. Good atmosphere, great drinks selection, one of the town's livelier pubs

ACCOMMODATION

New Addition: Glenfield House, Corkickle, CA28 7TS
01946 691911 / 07973 310950 **See Page: 4**

Glenard Guest House, Inkerman Terr, Whitehaven, CA28 7TY
Run by: Mrs. E. Armstrong

Large detached family run Victorian Guest House set in its own grounds. Breakfasts from 6am for those wishing for an early start. Secure cycle storage. 0.25 miles from start of C2C. All rooms are en-suite. Firm cyclists' favourite, they have been looking after C2Cers since the route started in 1994.

Rooms: 2D, 2S, 2T, 3F.
Months open: all year
B&B: £37.
Eve meal: no.
Pk lunch: £4.50.
Distance from route: 0.25 miles.
Pub: 5 minutes walk.
01946 692249
info@glenard.co.uk
glenard.co.uk

Moresby Hall, Moresby, Whitehaven, Cumbria, CA28 6PJ
Run by: Jane & David Saxon

Grade I listed building dating from 1620, Moresby Hall retains its antique charm while offering up to date comfort. 'For a spot of luxury at the start, or your reward at end of the journey, our beautiful guest rooms and award winning breakfast (Visit Britain) will surely enhance your trip,' says Jane. Plenty of parking space, you can leave your car free of charge for the duration. Fully licensed with a selection of reasonably priced beers, wines and spirits, the excellent set menu changes daily. Two miles from Whitehaven, there are walled gardens. Children over 10 only.

Rooms: 8D/T (with family sharing possibilities).
B&B: from £60pp if sharing.
Single occ: £75-£90.
Eve meal: £25 for 2-courses during week; £32.50 for 3-courses Fri & Sat.
Secure cycle storage and drying facilities.
01946 696317
info@moresbyhall.co.uk
moresbyhall.co.uk

Chestnuts, Low Moresby, Whitehaven, Cumbria, CA28 6RX

Run by: Norah Messenger

Ideal family accommodation with children welcome, Chestnuts is also ideal if you're travelling up and planning to set off the next day. 'A brilliant start to our C2C,' reported one rider on Trip Advisor. In a small quiet, village two miles from Whitehaven. Guestrooms are top end. Substantial breakfasts and packed lunches if required. Secure overnight cycle storage and parking for your car for the duration of your ride. Local pub 5 minutes by footpath (or car) and captive owls to visit during your stay and to hoot you on your way!

Rooms: 2 D en-suite, adjoining children's room for up to 16 years, price on application. Open all year.

B&B: £40 (£45 single occ)

Pk lunch: from £5. Secure cycle parking.

Distance from route: 2 miles from start (on Reivers route).

Pub: 5 minutes walk along footpath.

01946 61612 \ 07800 538298

owlmagic@sky.com

chestnuts-whitehaven.com

Chase Hotel, Inkerman Terrace, Whitehaven CA28 8AA

Run by: Alan Graham

You can leave your car here for the duration of the ride. Good for groups, Chase is a privately owned Victorian former gentleman's residence in two acres of grounds. Quiet and comfortable with plenty of parking space, yet only a short stroll from the town centre. There is a secure lock-up for bikes (they have been looking after C2Cers since the route opened). Special £50 dinner, bed and breakfast deals for groups. £38pp (£2 discount) Fri/Sat/Sun for groups. Please call to arrange.

Rooms: 23. 6S, 4T, 13D.

B&B: from £38 (discounted rate Fri/Sat/Sun only). Otherwise £40-£55pp. D,B&B £50.

Eve meal: £7 - £15. 2-courses £15.

Pk lunch: from £5

Fully licensed: 0.25 miles from route. Town centre. Car parking for duration.

01946 693656 / 01946 590807

info@chasewhitehaven.co.uk

chasewhitehaven.co.uk

Summergrove Halls, Hensingham, Whitehaven Cumbria CA28 8XZ

Run by: Joanne Arthur

More much needed accommodation at the most popular start-point, Summergrove has 131 double rooms just 2 miles from the centre of town. Book room only and add meals as required or choose self-catering. Free car parking and an in-house gym, beautiful surroundings. Quote C2C on booking and get a 10% discount.

Rooms: 131D/S (three-quarter size beds) with en-suite shower rooms.

Room only: £30.00;

Room with shared beverage kitchen £32.00, self-catered with shared kitchen £34.00. **Full English breakfast:** £5.00.

Eve meal: yes - large dining room.

Pk lunch: by prior arrangement.

Secure cycle storage and drying facilities.

01946 813328

info@summergrovehalls.co.uk

summergrovehalls.co.uk

CLEATOR & ENNERDALE

Ennerdale village spans the River Ehen and is close to Ennerdale Water, the most westerly of the lakes (and the most remote - it is the only lake which has no road running alongside). Here lies one of the largest forests in Cumbria in the Ennerdale Valley, with more than 20 miles of forest road plus a tangle of footpaths open to the public. The village is only a short hop from the C2C (also known as the West Cumbria Cyclepath). Wainwright's Coast to Coast Walk travels through Cleator before reaching Ennerdale village.

Forged in the furnace heat of old technology, Cleator Moor is a creation of the Industrial Revolution. The era's insatiable need for more coal, limestone and iron ore meant that the village became a town, which developed rapidly in the 19th century. As did the villages around it: Frizington, Rowrah, Keekle, Bigrigg produced the raw materials for iron works in Cleator Moor and Workington. To service this hive of industrial activity there was also an intricate network of railways, known as the Cleator & Workington junction railway.

ST BEES

St Bees to Keswick: 28 miles

By popular request we decided in 2007 to introduce a third possible start to the route. St Bees is the tried and trusted start to the Coast to Coast walk, famously founded by Alfred Wainwright in 1973. It is also a lovely coastal setting and a splendid but smaller alternative to the bustling charms of Whitehaven and Workington.

▶ DIRECTIONS

St Bees to merge point with Whitehaven route

- Those arriving at St Bees by train should leave the station to the Priory Church side and make their way along the 'Coach Road' past the petrol station and garage to the beach.
St Bees Head is the most westerly point in the North of England and on a clear day from the promenade you can look out to the Isle of Man, 20 miles or so off the coast.

- The first stage of the route takes you to Egremont, four miles away. Leave the beach car park and take the first right along the straight road to the Station. Cross the level crossing and continue up the Main Street past the Platform 9 restaurant and the Queen's Hotel on your right, the Manor House Hotel and the post office on your left.
- At the next junction you have the choice to take:
  The challenging route left up Outrigg (20%) and over Baybarrow, with rewarding views over to Ennerdale, Wasdale and down the coast to Eskdale and further
- Or continue up the Main Street to take the second right – signposted for the Hadrian's Cycleway C72 route – and follow the coast (Nethertown Road) and charming single-track lanes to Coulderton, then head inland for Egremont and the Lakes.
- At the T-junction in Coulderton head right to Middletown, taking first left just before the telephone box. Follow the lane for a short while, but instead of heading right, go straight on past Black Ling and Pickett How, up the narrow minor road. Make sure to enjoy views across to Dent Fell – the western edge of the Lake District as you head towards Egremont. Arriving in Egremont, take time to visit the Castle (pictured), then follow the national cycle route 72 which is clearly signed through the town and out to the north.

- About a mile north of Egremont is Clintz Quarry Nature Reserve, a limestone quarry of dramatic proportions with 100ft cliffs. It is home to some rare orchids in May and June, and is a sanctuary for birds.

 ## ACCOMMODATION

Queen's Hotel, Main St, St Bees, Cumbria, CA27 0DE
Run by: Mark Smedley

The project to refurbish this 17th century inn is now complete and there are now more rooms. The Queen's has a cosy country pub atmosphere, with oak beams and log fires. There are two real ale bars and a decent wine list. The restaurant has been stylishly redesigned and all meals are cooked on the premises using locally sourced ingredients where possible. Large conservatory and terraced garden. Secure cycle storage.

Rooms: 3S, 4T, 1F, 5D.
B&B: £27.50-£55.
Eve meal: from £6.95.
Pk lunch: from £4.95.
01946 822287
enquiries@queenshotelstbees.co.uk
queenshotelstbees.co.uk

Fairladies Barn Guest House, Main St, St Bees, Cumbria CA27 0AD
Run by: Will & Nicola Corrie
Luxury accommodation at affordable prices in an attractive converted
17th century sandstone barn, which stands back from the upper end
of the high street, with a sun trap garden area. Fairladies looks as if it
has been transported from one of those picture postcard villages in the
Dordogne. Secure lock-up in a shed, but cyclists welcome to take bikes to
their rooms.
Rooms: 4D, 3T, 2F
(1D & 1T with shared bathroom)
B&B: £32.50. £45 single.
Eve meal: Lots of nearby pubs.
Pk lunch: £6.
01946 822718
info@fairladiesbarn.co.uk
fairladiesbarn.co.uk

LORTON

▶ DIRECTIONS

Merging of the routes to Lorton

- Whether you have come up the disused
  railway line from Whitehaven or joined
  the main cycle route from St Bees, the
  next stage sees you cut through Cleator
  Moor and rejoin the old railway heading
  towards Rowrah and Kirkland.

- Beyond Rowrah turn left onto the lane
  and right at the school. You will soon
  pass Felldyke where you follow the signs
  for Lamplugh and Loweswater.

- In about 5km you will be skirting
  Loweswater, your first glimpse of the
  Lakes and a wonderful spot to take
  pictures.

- The bridge over the Cocker at Low
  Lorton is repaired and the route has
  returned to normal and is clearly
  signposted.

- *There is nothing stopping you taking
  the alternative route via Loweswater,
  Scalehill Birdge and the B5289 to
  Lorton.*

ON ARRIVAL

Alfred Wainwright, Britain's most famous walking hero and pioneer of the outdoors, regarded this area, with its deeply gouged valleys reached from the passes of Whinlatter, Honister and Newlands, as his favourite spot.

Lorton is only about 5km south of Cockermouth, so it is also an optional diversion for those who have decided to start their journey from Workington.

To reach New House (see P36) on the B5289: Carry on straight through Loweswater for 3km on the road parallel with the route:
Turn right onto the B5289 at the cross-roads just beyond the Lorton bridge. It's only 2km from the route.

 ## ACCOMMODATION

Meadow Bank, High Lorton, Cockermouth, Cumbria CA13 9UG
Run by: Christine Edmunds
The reception here is as warm as the rooms and the location could hardly be bettered. Secure bike storage, drying facilities - pub close by and a great breakfast to see you on your way.
Rooms: 1D, 1T (en-suite)
B&B: £30 - £32.
Pk Lunch: £4.
Distance from C2C: 300m.
Pub: 1 km.
01900 85315
CEdm85315@aol.com
buttermerecumbria.com

New House Farm, Lorton, Cockermouth, Cumbria CA139UU

Run by: Hazel Thompson

Recession busting deals possible. Consult the website or, better still, call Hazel to see what's on offer. Easy route: ignore left turn for Thackthwaite and continue over Scalehill Bridge and take the alternative (and more attractive) route to Lorton. 'Winning 17th century grade II listed farmhouse set in stunning surroundings, now boasting a tearoom with delicious home-made produce. Beautiful antiques throughout complement the original oak beams, flag floors and stone fireplaces where log fires crackle on colder days. Four posters, hot tub in the garden. Delicious food.'

Rooms: 5D, 1T (E-S).
B&B: £80 (see above).
Pk Lunch: £7.50.
Eve meal: £30 for 3 courses.
Distance from C2C: on alternative parallel route.
VisitBritain 5 stars
Which? Hotel of the year award winner.
Pub 2km. Tearoom available.
01900 85404 \ 07841 159818
enquiries@newhouse-farm.co.uk
newhouse-farm.com

OVER WHINLATTER

▶ DIRECTIONS

- The first real challenge comes when you leave High Lorton: the uphill slog to Whinlatter, the first section of which is unremitting, until you join the B5292 on the Whinlatter Pass.

- You should bear right along the forest track, then first left along the wide track, ignoring other routes to the right. This takes you over rough terrain for a couple of kilometres before coming out on the B5292, at which point go left then right for the Whinlatter Visitor Centre (if for any reason the off-road track is closed, as it was when I last cycled the C2C, continue along the road to the visitor centre).

- Of course, feel free just to take the road. It's quicker and easier, but there is traffic and if you're on a road bike avoid the off-road here as it is proper off-road, as opposed to 'traffic-free.'

- Beyond the visitor centre the route goes sharp right down a forest track to Thornthwaite, commanding some stunning views of Bassenthwaite Lake.

- If you opt to continue down the winding road take good care. It is steep, narrow and cars come up and down with varying degrees of road awareness.

- There is now an extensive range of mountain bike routes and Whinlatter is fast becoming the hub for northern Lakeland off-roading.

- Also leave yourself enough time to have a good look around the visitor centre. There's a wealth of forest habitat information, a fine tea room and shop.

- Take time, weather permitting, to admire Blencathra, Skiddaw and, over to the right, Helvellyn. You are in the heart of England's only mountain forest. Because of the pure mountain air a sanatorium used to stand in the Whinlatter Forest. Sailors with TB and other communicable diseases were kept there in isolation.

forestry.gov.uk/whinlatterhome | 017687 78469

- After Thornthwaite the route links up with the Workington to Keswick alternative, via Braithwaite and Portinscale, where there are some charming accommodation possibilities.

Legend:
- Route
- Traffic-Free Section
- Wiggo's Way Loop
- Weardale Alternative
- Durham Loop
- 10km grid

A66

Troutbeck

Threlkeld

Keswick

Derwent Water

Bassenthwaite Lake

Thornwaite

A66

Lorton

Loweswater

A595

A596

A5086

Cockermouth

A66

Maryport

Cleator Moor

Workington

Whitehaven

WORKINGTON → KESWICK

Workington to Keswick: 24 miles (5 miles traffic-free)

WORKINGTON

▶ DEPARTURE ROUTE

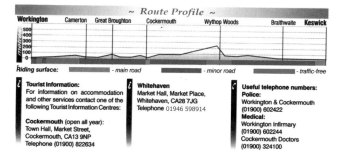

~ Route Profile ~

| Workington | Camerton | Great Broughton | Cockermouth | Wythop Woods | Braithwaite | Keswick |

Riding surface: ████ - main road   ████ - minor road   ████ - traffic-free

Tourist Information:
For information on accommodation and other services contact one of the following Tourist Information Centres:

Cockermouth (open all year):
Town Hall, Market Street,
Cockermouth, CA13 9NP
Telephone (01900) 822634

Whitehaven
Market Hall, Market Place,
Whitehaven, CA28 7JG
Telephone 01946 598914

Useful telephone numbers:
Police:
Workington & Cockermouth
(01900) 602422
Medical:
Workington Infirmary
(01900) 602244
Cockermouth Doctors
(01900) 324100

ABOUT THE TOWN

Alongside some splendid Georgian architecture is some powerful industrial heritage to reflect the fact that Workington is an ancient market and erstwhile industrial boom town. At the mouth of the River Derwent, parts of it date back to Roman times. But it was not until the 18th century, with the exploitation of local iron ore and coal, that Workington expanded to become a major industrial port. Having once provided the steel for nearly every country in the world's railway lines, this grand old bruiser of a town fell into decline but with the help of European funding in 2007, its centre has gradually come back to life.

Workington's growth mirrors that of its neighbour, Whitehaven, eight miles down the coast. Iron and steel manufacturing have always been at the heart of life here, and it was in this town that Henry Bessemer first introduced his revolutionary steel making process, florally commemorated in this picture. In recent years, with the decline of the steel industry and coal mining, the town has had to diversify and with the refurbishment of the town centre it is ready to welcome tourists to its heart. The advantage of starting here is that the opening leg of the journey is seven miles shorter, has gentler gradients and passes through the Georgian market town of Cockermouth. It is also close to, and goes through, Camerton, where the church sits prettily on the banks of the Derwent. It has some nice churches. The parish church of St Michael's has been on its present site since the 7th century, although the 12th century Norman church was replaced in 1770 by a larger building. Sadly this was severely damaged by fire in 1994, but has since undergone a major rebuilding programme. St John's Church was built in 1823 to commemorate the battle of Waterloo, to a design by Thomas Hardwick. It is built of local sandstone, and bears some resemblance to Inigo Jones's St Paul's Church in Covent Garden, London.

Workington Tourist Information Centre 016973 31944

CYCLE SHOPS

Bike Bank, 18-20 Market Place. 01900 603 337
Halfords, Derwent Howe Retail Park. 01900 601 635

🔭 PLACES OF INTEREST

Workington Hall

Workington Hall is built around a pele tower dating from the 14th century, and was once one of the finest manor houses in the region.

This striking ruin, once owned by the Curwen family, Lords of the Manor of Workington, gave shelter to Mary Queen of Scots on her last flight from Scotland before her imprisonment and execution.

It is said to be haunted by Henry Curwen, who sank the nearby Jane Pit in the 19th century, the remains of which can be seen at nearby Mossbay.

Town Museum

The Helena Thompson Museum was bequeathed to the people of Workington by the eponymous Miss Thompson, a local philanthropist, in 1940. It houses displays of pottery, silver, glass, and furniture dating from Georgian times, as well as the social and industrial history of Workington and the surrounding area.

🍴 WHERE TO EAT

SUPERFISH, 20 Pow St. Sit-in or takeaway. 01900 604916
BLUE DOLPHIN, 1 Lismore Place. Sit-in or takeaway. 01900 604114
THE PURPLE CHERRY, 26 Finkle Street. 01900 871752
NEW BENGAL SPICE, 39 Jane St. 01900 64106

Morven House Hotel, Siddick Road, Workington, Cumbria CA14 1LE

Run by: Mrs Caroline Nelson

Right at the start of the C2C and close to the finish of the Reivers, the Morven is relaxed and well fit for purpose. All bedrooms are en-suite, comfortable. Large detached house with car park and secure cycle storage. You can leave your cars until you return if you wish.

Rooms: 2D, 6T (all en-suite).

B&B: £33-£38. For groups of 6 or more: £30.
Deposit of £20 per person required

Pk lunch: £6.

Eve meal: £10-£12.

On route. VisitBritain 3 stars. Pub nearby.

01900 602118

cnelsonmorven@aol.com

morvenguesthouse.com

Armidale Cottages, 29 High Seaton, CA14 1PD

Run by: Sue Dahl

Just a few hundred yards from the track and five minutes from the start/ finish, Armidale is set in half an acre of land with a small orchard. The cottage has wood burning stoves in the lounge and dining room and is centrally heated throughout. There are slate floors in the lounge and hall with wood floors in the dining room and bedroom. Great breakfast and top end accommodation. Credit cards now accepted. Also handy for Hadrian's Cycleway. You can leave up to 2 cars here while doing the route.

Rooms: 2D.

B&B: £35-£43. single occ.

Pk lunch: on request.

Local inspection: Commended.

01900 63704 / 07771768423

armidalecotts@hotmail.com

armidalecottages.co.uk

Waverley Hotel

Run by: Lynn & Del Pears

The owners have been running the Waverley, this bike-friendly town centre hotel for 27 years. Recently refurbished and comfortable it is ideal for groups, as there are 27 rooms. Secure cycle storage and you can opt for a packed lunch instead of breakfast. Ideal stop-off in a town well worth exploring.

Rooms: 12T, 9D, 6S.

B&B: from £45.

Pk lunch: £6 (or you can have it instead of breakfast)

Eve Meal: full bar menu from snacks to steaks.
3-course dinner for £10.50.

01900 65892

waverley-hotel@btconnect.com

waverley-hotel.com

COCKERMOUTH

Cockermouth is one of the most attractive towns in the northwest and is one of only two places in the Lakes to be designated a 'Gem Town' 40 years ago. That means it is protected and will, in essence, remain the same in perpetuity.

It is just outside the boundary of the Lake District National Park and perhaps for this reason is not inundated with tourists and the tackiness that often goes with the industry.

It developed at the confluence of two great salmon rivers – the Cocker, which flows out of lakes Buttermere, Crummock and Loweswater; and the Derwent, which runs through Derwentwater and Bassenthwaite Lake to Workington.

The town got its market charter in 1221, and has retained its importance over the centuries. Later there was quarrying and mining for lead and iron outside the town, and a brewery at the foot of the castle mound, where the two rivers meet.

It has long fascinated writers, poets and artists and is the birthplace of William and Dorothy Wordsworth – one of the finest buildings here is Wordsworth House, pictured above, the Lakeland poet's family home, which is now in the care of the National Trust.

The great architectural guru Sir Nikolaus Pevsner, in his 'Buildings of England', described the place as 'quite a swagger house for such a town'. Built in 1745 for the then High Sheriff of Cumberland, Joshua Lucock, it was bought in 1761 by Sir James Lowther, son of Sir John, who built Whitehaven and its port. John Wordsworth, the poet's father, moved to Cockermouth as agent to Sir James in 1764, and in 1766 married and moved into the house. Here four sons and a daughter were born. Their mother died when William was eight, and he went to live with relations in Penrith.

The house thrived as a private residence until 1937, when it was put on the market. Since it was in a prime location in the centre of town, bosses of the local bus company snapped it up as the natural spot for a bus station. They applied for – and got – planning permission to bulldoze it, but there was such a national outcry that funds were raised for the town to buy it back and hand it over to the National Trust. The old kitchen and the housekeeper's room now serve as a café/restaurant where you can get morning coffee, light lunches and afternoon tea. Two other famous men were born in Eaglesfield, a mile from the town's centre: Fletcher Christian, the man who led the mutiny on the Bounty was born in 1764, and attended the same school as Wordsworth; then in 1766 came John Dalton, a brilliant scientist and originator of atomic theory.

Cockermouth Castle was built in the 13th century, but not much of it remains because of the efforts of Robert the Bruce and his marauding Scots. Most of the remaining ruins are from a later period, between 1360 and 1370.

🔭 PLACES OF INTEREST

Jennings Brewery
Offers 1½ hour tours around its premises, pictured below, explaining the processes involved in brewing traditional beer.
0845 1297185,
jenningsbrewery.co.uk

The Bitter End, 15 Kirkgate
Reopened by popular demand in 2011 – 'Cumbria's Smallest Brewery'.
01900 828993
bitterend.co.uk.

Castle Brewery, home of Cumbria's best known brewers – Jennings.
Photo by Jim Hardman.

Lakeland Sheep & Wool Centre
01900 822673
At the roundabout on the A66 is where you can meet
Cumbria's most famous residents.

Castlegate House
Contemporary art exhibitions.
01900 822149

Tourist Information Centre
Town Hall, Market Place, Cockermouth, CA13 9NP
01900 822634

WHERE TO EAT

BEATFORDS COUNTRY RESTAURANT, 7 Lowther Went.
Popular tearoom. Good simple food. 01900 827099

TARANTELLA, 22 Main St,
Cockermouth, Cumbria CA13
9LQ. Bustling, high quality
Italian. 01900 822109

**THE BITTER END BREW
PUB**, 15 Kirkgate. Excellent
value, great beer and great
food. 01900 828993

QUINCE & MEDLAR, 13
Castlegate. One of the best
vegetarian restaurants in Britain,
featured in the Good Food Guide.
Wood panelling, soft candle light,
next to the castle. 01900 823579

NORHAM COFFEE HOUSE & RESTAURANT, 73 Main St
01900 824330

CARLINS BISTRO BAR, Allerdale Hotel, 18-20 Market Place.
01900 823654

LEE'S CHINESE TAKEAWAY AND FISH & CHIPS, 47 Main
St. Expert fish friers. 01900 827770

THE SPICE CLUB, 25 Main St. Upmarket Indian cuisine for
reasonable prices. Underwent major renovations. 01900
828288

Embleton Spa Hotel, Embleton, Near Cockermouth, CA13 9XU
Run by: Alastair Dixon

Pretty much bang on the route between Cockermouth and Keswick, this is a great location close to Bassenthwaite Lake and in the middle of the Fells. It's ideal for groups up to 40, offering en-suite double rooms and apartment-style suites for up to 8 adults. You can unwind in the spa after a day in the saddle and eat in the bar or bistro. Great seasonal local ingredients imaginatively cooked by an experienced kitchen. Hot tubs and views of Skiddaw, Sale Fell and Ling Fell. Ideal for back-up teams wishing to chill out.

B&B: £50-£60pppn.
Rooms: 12. 6D (2 of which are apartments);
1F (1D+2S);
2F apartments (1D+2S+kitchen)
plus 2 apartments which each sleep 5
and a 3-bed apartment which sleeps 8.
Lunch: 12-2.30.
Eve meal: 6-9.
3-courses between £25-£30.
017687 76606
enquiries@embletonspa.co.uk
embletonspa.co.uk

Riverside, 12 Market St, Cockermouth, Cumbria, CA13 9NJ
Run by: Rachel Habgood

Georgian home with comfortable beds, excellent breakfasts, local amenities, tea-trays and drying facilities plus bike lock-up. Short walk to the local bike shop and town centre where there are excellent pubs and restaurants. Free wifi.

Rooms: 2T, 1S.
B&B: £30-35.
Pk lunch: £5.
Dist from route: right on C2C & Reivers.
Pubs: lots of choice nearby.
01900 827504
riversidebedandbreakfast.co.uk

THORNTHWAITE

▶ DIRECTIONS

Leaving Cockermouth and on to Thornthwaite

- Cross over Gote Street from the Papcastle road and continue past the James Walker factory, then right onto Bridge Street, crossing the river just after the doctor's surgery.
- You then head left onto Main Street. Go past Station Street before turning right into Challoner Street, left into Cocker Lane and then almost immediately right to follow the river. Go under Lorton Street towards the Youth Hostel, turn right to swivel over the River Cocker and follow the path past the cemetery before the hairpin right turn onto Strawberry Home Road, where you take a left. It is now a straightforward run.

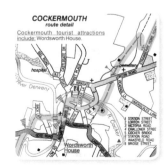

- You may wish to stop near the shores of Bassenthwaite's northern tip, in which case go through the village of Wythop Mill and turn right by the phone box.
- Turn left at the Pheasant Inn and go over the A66 onto the B5291,taking the scenic Ouse

Bridge to the Castle Hotel. After that, it's a short hop along the road and up to the village and the Sun Inn, where they serve good food and ale. Assuming you do not opt for this diversion, you will encounter a short, hilly section before the descent to Bassenthwaite Lake, from whence it is an easy ride into Keswick. At Thornthwaite you meet up with the Whitehaven route.

LEGEND OF BARF AND THE BISHOP

There is a Viking burial ground here at Powter Howe and just behind it is a hill called Barf.

You will see two large white rocks – one halfway up Barf, one at the bottom. The higher one is the Bishop, and the lower the Clerk. They commemorate the tale of a deadly 18th century drinking session at the Swan Inn (now transformed into holiday apartments) during which the bibulous Bishop of Londonderry (doubtless on diocesan duty) bet his clerk that he could ride his horse to the top of Barf. They downed their glasses and set off. The Right Reverend fell and broke his neck half-way up, while the clerk never collected his winnings. The stones are said to commemorate this foolhardy wager. I do not know whether the bishop and his horse were on their way up or down when they fell and await enlightenment from an informed reader.

Thornthwaite overlooks Bassenthwaite Lake, the only 'lake' in the Lake District. This may seem strange, but all the other expanses of H2O in the so-called Lake District are Waters, Meres or Tarns.

 ## ACCOMMODATION

Lanefoot Farm, Thornthwaite, Nr Keswick, CA12 5RZ
Run by: Helen and Gareth Davies
Informal but lovely camping set-up, superb location, offering a studio flat (sleeps 2) plus a Family Camping Pod from £43 a night, plus two standard Camping Pods (from £37) and a Shepherd's Hut complete with electricity, each sleeping two adults comfortably. Bang on the route with decent facilities at good prices. There are a couple of fields, plenty of space and a proper country feel, within easy striking distance of pubs and restaurants. Now has an online booking facility.
Studio: £27.50pp per night.
Camping Pods & Shepherd's Hut:
from £37 per night.
Camping: please email or call to book, or alternatively book online via our website.
017687 78097
helen@stayinthornthwaite.co.uk
stayinthornthwaite.co.uk

Powter Howe, Thornthwaite, Braithwaite, nr Keswick, CA12 5SQ
Run by: Karen Lockwoood
Comfortable and friendly bed and breakfast accommodation within a
beautiful 16th Century period farmhouse property set in two acres of
mature gardens in a beautiful rural location overlooking Bassenthwaite
Lake. A warm welcome awaits with an open fire in the guest lounge.
Accommodation comprises two double bedrooms (one en-suite), one
twin and single rooms available upon request. A hearty home cooked
breakfast using locally sourced produce is provided - evening meals and
packed lunches by prior arrangement. Safe overnight bike store provided,
with a local frequent bus route within walking distance. Adjacent to the
route, ask about our C2C dinner and packed lunch deal.
Rooms: 2D (1 en-suite), 1T, S rooms available on request.
B&B: £30.
Eve meal: Yes - call to find out.
Pubs: 2 miles away in Braithwaite.
Pk lunch: by arrangement.
Open all year & dog friendly. On route.
Pub: 2 miles.
01768 778415
info@powter-howe.co.uk
powter-howe.co.uk

BRAITHWAITE

▶ DIRECTIONS

Convergence point of all 3 starts

- Nestling at the bottom of the Whinlatter Pass and Newlands Valley
  with the spectacular backdrop of Grisedale Pike and Bassenthwaite
  Lake, the routes from Whitehaven, St Bees and Workington merge
  in time to take you to the picturesque village of Braithwaite.

- Braithwaite is half-way between Thornthwaite and Keswick. It's an
  excellent base for touring the Lake District, close to Loweswater,
  Crummock Water and Buttermere.

- It's a straight and pleasant run through a quintessentially English
  village scene, over a medieval humped-back bridge. This section
  of Braithwaite, leading out towards Little Braithwaite and Ullock, is
  somehow preserved in time. Only cars spoil the scene – otherwise
  you could be back in the 18th century.

ACCOMMODATION

The Coledale Inn, Braithwaite, Nr Keswick, Cumbria CA12 5TN

Run by: Garry & Carole

The Coledale is a genuine country inn, really popular with cyclists, situated above Braithwaite Village in a peaceful hillside position, well away from passing traffic. It is ideal for cycling and walking, with paths to the mountains immediately outside the hotel gardens. Ideal spot to explore the area for those not in a rush. Now runs the White Horse at Scales. All 20 rooms completely refurbished and the beer garden has also had a makeover.

Rooms: 2S, 10D, 6T, 2F.
B&B: £35-£43 depending on time of year/deals on offer.
Eve meal: from £9.95.
Light snack/sandwiches: from £4.95.
Pk lunch: £5.
On route. VisitBritain 3-stars.
017687 78272
info@coledale-inn.co.uk
coledale-inn.co.uk

KESWICK

▶ DIRECTIONS

Braithwaite to Keswick

• The route to Keswick via Portinscale is well signposted. You come into the town up the main street, following the traffic to the left and up to the lights at the Penrith Road. If not stopping in this delightful town, then go left down Station Street, turn right onto Brundholme Road, round in a loop and pick up the track heading east.

Sandwiched between Derwentwater, Blencathra and Skiddaw at the entrance to the mighty Borrowdale valley, this market town is blessed with one of Britain's most idyllic settings.

It is ideal for cycling, walking, boating or just sightseeing, and is a favourite venue with cycle back-up teams; it is the most popular and best-equipped stop-off point on the route.

Keswick ('Cese-Wic' - the Cheese Town, literally) became prosperous in the 16th century, during the reign of Elizabeth I, thanks to copper, lead, silver and iron mining.

There was so much work that engineers had to be imported from Germany. Despite a rocky start – at one stage, local xenophobia drove them to inhabit Derwent Island – they soon managed to integrate; evidence of this can be found in the phone book today, with its many Germanic surnames.

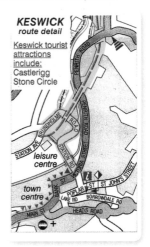

KESWICK
route detail

Keswick tourist attractions include:
Castlerigg Stone Circle

 CYCLE SHOPS

Keswick Mountain Bikes
for MTB, Road, Hybrid, e Bike, Childrens, Clothing, Accessories, Hire & Workshop.

Open 9.30am - 5.30pm 7 days

133 main Street Keswick, CA12 5NJ
017687 73355/75202

keswickmountainbikes.co.uk

To the Point

The town's Cumberland Pencil Company was established after the discovery of graphite in Borrowdale in the 16th century. However, the town was granted its charter some 300 years before that by Edward I in 1276. Visitors started to flock in during the 18th century and Victorian times. Many of them were literary pilgrims, attracted by the association with such Romantic poets as Southey, Coleridge and Wordsworth. John Ruskin, the aesthete and champion of the Pre-Raphaelites, had close associations with the town. The population of the place has grown little in the past century. In 1902 there were 4,500 people; now there are just 500 more, but many of them – as you will note if you choose to stop over – are B&B owners. The place also has many good pubs and reliable eateries.

PLACES OF INTEREST

The Cumberland Pencil Museum, West of the town centre.
017687 73626

The Keswick Launch Company, tours on the lake, on the shore of Derwentwater. 017687 72263

George Fisher, big stock of outdoor gear, books and maps. Borrowdale Rd. 017687 72178

Cotswold Outdoor Ltd, as above. 017687 81939

The Moot Hall, Tourist Information Centre. 017687 72645

Theatre by the Lake, Lakeside. Open all year round. Restaurant. Beautiful setting. 017687 74411

Alhambra Cinema, St.Johns St. 017687 72195

Castlerigg Stone Circle, thought to date from 3000 B.C. Steep climb out of town on the alternative Penrith Rd route. Worth the detour.

Keswick Museum & Art Gallery, Station Rd. 017687 72263
Tremendous Victorian collection. Has just reopened after major refurbishment.

WHERE TO EAT

SADDLEBACK CAFE, 135 Main St, Keswick, CA12 5NJ. 017687 73907. Great new resource next to Keswick Mountain Bike shop. High praise for the breakfast deal consisting of a 'door stop' sandwich with a choice of sausage, bacon and egg (or a bit of all three) and either tea or coffee for £4.75. Good value and nicely cooked and presented. Selection of hot and cold drinks and cakes. Cycling themes in the cafe but open for all. Friendly staff. Outdoor seating area. Andy & Sarah West.

CAFE 26, 26 Lake Road. Good wines, tasty Italian/ Spanish style lunches. Tapas Thurs, Fri & Sat nights. 4 guest rooms. 017687 80863

STRADA ITALIAN BISTRO, 31 Lake Road. International cuisine with tapas, pizzas and other family favourites: 017687 73088

SALSA MEXICAN BISTRO, 1 New Street. Spicy and popular medium priced establishment owned by the Nellist brothers: 017687 75222

SWINSIDE INN, Newlands, Keswick 017687 78253

LUCA'S RISTORANTE, High Hill, Greta Bridge.
Family run Italian with elaborate decorations
and prices to match: 017687 74621

THE BANK TAVERN, 47 Main St. Solid, handsome
pub with good, traditional English cooking. Medium
price. Outside eating area: 017687 72663

GEORGE HOTEL, 3 St John St. Medium priced fare:
017687 75751

Ancient Stone Circle of Castlerigg at Keswick

 ## ACCOMMODATION

Denton House, Penrith Rd, Keswick, CA12 4JW
Run by: Libby Scott
Friendly purpose built hostel that is happy to provide outdoor activities
for those wanting it, but more than happy to provide beds for those
wishing to crash out after a hard day's cycling. This is budget bunk bed
accommodation and there is secure bike storage and a drying room. It is a
5 minute walk into town. Group bookings welcome by arrangement. There
are 65 beds so large groups welcome. You can book the whole place
Rooms: 8 containing 65 bunk beds.
Bed: £17 during week. £19 weekends.
(with £5 supplement for 1-nighters Fri & Sat)
For use of whole centre (weekdays): £850.
Whole centre (weekends): £950.
Food for Groups of 15 or more: £3.75.
Pk lunch: £6 (baguette and calorific munchies).
Eve meal: £10 for 2-course, all locally sourced.
Pub 200m: on route.
01768 775351
keswickhostel@hotmail.co.uk
dentonhouse-keswick.co.uk

Cranford House, 18 Eskin St, Keswick, CA12 4DG

Run by: Carol Hallgarth

Great value town centre B&B just a couple of minutes from the pubs and restaurants. Carol runs a cycle-friendly, doily-free house that makes up for in comfort what it lacks in chintz. Safe lock-up, drying facilities and all that you need for a comfortable stop-off after a day in the saddle.

Rooms: 2S, 3T/D, 1D.

B&B: £33 for single with shared bathroom.
£36pp for en-suite twin & doubles

Pk lunch: £5.50.

01768 771017
carol@cranfordhouse.co.uk
cranfordhouse.co.uk

Twa Dogs Inn, Penrith Rd, Keswick, CA12 4JU

Run by: Peter & Marjorie Harding & family

Good beer, good food and a comfortable bed probably explains why this is a truly popular stop-off with C2Cers. It is fast becoming one of the main stop-offs in bustling Keswick. This is a traditional, no-nonsense family run concern with an atmosphere as warm as the welcome. Open fires, dominoes, darts & pool in a proper pub. Lock-up for bikes and a range of real ales for their owners. Meal deal: £2.50pp off evening meal for those booking accommodation by phone.

Rooms: 3T/D, 1T, 1F (2S & 1D). All en-suite.

B&B: £35. Kids negotiable.

Eve meal: from £8.25.

Pk lunch: £5.

Distance from C2C: Just above the railway line coming out of Keswick.

01768 772599
twadogsinn@aol.co.uk
twadogs.co.uk

Springs Farm, Springs Rd, Keswick, CA12 4AN

Run by: Hazel Hutton

Comfortable accommodation in a large 19th century farmhouse at the foot of Walla Crag. Also has a farmhouse shop and tea room. This is a working dairy farm offering quality accommodation in an idyllic location. It is a 10 minute walk into town. This has been home to the Hutton family since 1924 and remains an entirely family operated business to this day. There is a pretty courtyard with ample parking. To the rear is a large orchard with apple, pear and plum trees, where free-range hens lay your breakfast eggs. And now there's a satellite TV, too. There are also 3 cottages sleeping 6, 2 and 2. Satellite TV available throughout.

Rooms: 2D, 1T.

B&B: £36.50-£42.

Nearest pub: 1 mile to town centre. AA 4-star accommodation for self-catering cottages; AA 3-star for B&B. Safe lock up. Cleaning facilities. Tea room and farmhouse shop opening at Easter.
01768 772144 / 07816 824253
springsfarmkeswick@gmail.com
springs-farm.co.uk

KESWICK → LANGWATHBY

28 miles (6 miles traffic-free)

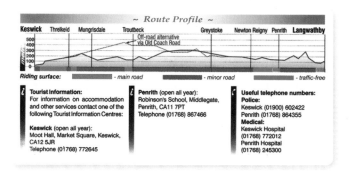

~ Route Profile ~

Keswick   Threlkeld   Mungrisdale   Troutbeck   Greystoke   Newton Reigny   Penrith   Langwathby

Off-road alternative
via Old Coach Road

Riding surface: ▬▬▬▬ - main road   ▬▬▬▬ - minor road   ▬▬▬ - traffic-free

i **Tourist Information:**
For information on accommodation and other services contact one of the following Tourist Information Centres:

Keswick (open all year):
Moot Hall, Market Square, Keswick, CA12 5JR
Telephone (01768) 772645

i **Penrith** (open all year):
Robinson's School, Middlegate, Penrith, CA11 7PT
Telephone (01768) 867466

i **Useful telephone numbers:**
Police:
Keswick (01900) 602422
Penrith (01768) 864355
Medical:
Keswick Hospital
(01768) 772012
Penrith Hospital
(01768) 245300

▶ DIRECTIONS & ROUTE CHOICES

● There are two ways out of Keswick. The most popular – and by far the easier – is the traffic-free one that follows the old Keswick-Penrith railway line and the river Greta as far as Threlkeld. It is a beautiful and leafy stretch. You get to it down Station Road and Brundholme Road, bearing left at the swimming pool and heading in front of the old station.

● The alternative takes you up into the hills above the town, but is only for the fit. And you need a MTB, whereas the alternative can easily be tackled on a road bike.

● Both routes assume the same start (unless you want to go out of Keswick along the old Penrith road).

Up hill and up dale

If you're feeling energetic and (seriously) fit, try the Old Coach Road over the hills. It branches from the railway route, just before the track goes under the A66 viaduct, and goes up the steep slope to Castlerigg Stone Circle. Press on through St John's in the Vale, Matterdale End and down to Greystoke via Hutton John.

The Coach Road (what coach could possibly have tackled this?) is a seriously rough off-road alternative and very exposed. Check the weather before tackling it and don't do it if you're not certain of your capabilities.

The middle way

Start along the tougher route described above, but, after stopping to admire the Castlerigg Stone Circle, bear left down the hill and rejoin the more sedate option. Fine for road bikes.

Easy riding

This takes you fairly effortlessly alongside the River Greta, all the way to Threlkeld.

THRELKELD & SCALES

ABOUT THRELKELD

History from hunting to mining and back

Blencathra, known locally as Saddleback, overlooks this traditional and pretty village. There are also views towards Clough Head and the Helvellyn range.

Threlkeld is, apparently, Norse for 'the spring of the thrall' – thrall being a bonded servant. Zinc, lead and granite were mined during the last century until the last of the granite miners hung up their shovels and picks in the mid-80s.

At one time more than a hundred men were employed in the mines and at the quarry there is a museum with an impressive mineral collection, mining artefacts and touching reminders of how things used to be.

A table top relief map of the Lake District and a pictorial history of Threlkeld are also on display. There was once a TB isolation hospital which is now a field centre for biologists and geographers.

Since the Dark Ages and the days of Sir Lancelot de Threlkeld, hunting has been an integral part of local life; this is the home of the Blencathra Hunt, one of the lakeland packs that hunt on foot rather than on horseback and claims that its hounds are descended from those used by John Peel of song fame.

The Threlkeld sheepdog trials are a highlight of the year and feature foxhound and terrier shows, as well as hound trailing. All of these rural pursuits are, one presumes, still flourishing these days.

🍴 WHERE TO EAT

Threlkeld Coffee Shop, Threlkeld Village Hall, Keswick, Cumbria CA12 4RX
Run by: Paulo Resende
Threlkeld Village Hall, which houses this splendid new resource, is bang on the route. Commanding great views of Blencathra and the surrounding area the coffee shop has outside seating as well, and is a great place to stop for locally-sourced food and Fairtrade teas and coffees. Profits from Threlkeld Coffee Shop are used for the benefit of the local community. Offering lots of delicious baked produce, sandwiches, scones and soft drinks, there is also a shop.
1 March - 30 September :
Open 10am - 5pm every day.
Winter Opening:
Open 10am - 5pm Tuesday - Sunday.
Closed Mondays.
017687 79501
threlkeldcoffeeshop@btconnect.com
threlkeldvillagehall.org/coffeeshop

SCALES

Next Stop Scales

After Threlkeld there is a short section along a car-free country road, then a cycle path alongside the A66 until Scales, before you go along a delightful gated lane to Mungrisdale. Don't forget to look up to admire Blencathra on your left and the Helvellyn range to the right.

White Horse, Scales, Cumbria CA12 4SY

Run by: Geoff & Charlie Mawdsley

In the shadow of Blencathra, the White Horse Inn is a quintessential Country Pub with great food, open fires, local ales and a warm welcome. Just a mile beyond Threlkeld, the mountains start where the beer garden finishes. Now with accommodation for Hikers and C2C Cyclists - The White Horse Inn Bunkhouse has been converted from the stables of this traditional Lake District Inn. Four of the stables have been converted into bedrooms, one sleeping 4, two sleeping 6 in bunks and one sleeping 8. All centrally heated. Kitchen, dryer, dining room, pub. To book please call Charlie on 017687 79883 and view the website below for more information.

Bunkhouse: sleeps 24 man bunkhouse (1x8 man, 2x6 man, 1x4 man).
Bed: £10pppn. Sole occ of bunkhouse: £200.
Bedding: £5.
Kitchen, Dryer, Dining Room, Pub, Centrally Heated.
Meals: Snacks, sandwiches and full meals at lunch. Drinks served all day.
Dinner: 6-9pm. Main courses £9-£12.
017687 79883
info@thewhitehorse-blencathra.co.uk
thewhitehorse-blencathra.co.uk

MUNGRISDALE/ TROUTBECK

The village of Mungrisdale comprises a traditional inn, a church and a cluster of houses huddled around the river Glenderamackin. A truly restful spot, you reach it along the gated road from which there are spectacular views of the fells. Souther and Blencathra lie to the West and the Ullswater fells to the South whilst to the east the daunting prospect of the Pennines loom imposingly.

- The Sustrans route suggests you cross the river just short of the village, but that would be a shame. There is an alternative exit path over minor lanes, through Berrier and onto the Greystoke road, or follow the lane back down the other side of the Glenderamackin to the A66, where the cycle path takes over.

- At the top of the hill you can follow the route to the left or carry straight on for Greystoke. Either will do.

- Troutbeck is about two miles further along the A66 once you have returned to it from Mungrisdale.

Be very careful crossing, though. Many a motorist attempts the land speed record on this stretch.

TROUTBECK & MATTERDALE

Just to the east of the A66 is Troutbeck. For overnights, Troutbeck now has Lane Head Farm as well as the Troutbeck Inn.

Those tackling the off-road section along the Old Coach Road from Keswick will come into Dockray and will either go a) left down the A5091 to rejoin the main route at Troutbeck, or b) continue to Matterdale End then on to Sparket Mill and Hutton John.

 ## ACCOMMODATION

Troutbeck Inn, Troutbeck, Penrith, CA11 0SJ
Run by: Rowan Mahon

A handy point mid-way between Keswick and Penrith, this is a cosy, comfortable and relaxed inn with a four star rating from the English tourist board. In addition to seven rooms there are three cottages. Dogs welcome. The owner is a chef who has cooked in the Channel Isles and the culinary influence is French, with much use of local produce. And it's jolly good...

Rooms: 1T, 1S, 5D.
B&B: £37.50-£55 (single occ).
Lunch: £7.50 (soup & sandwich) to around £15.50 (sirloin steak).
Eve meal: Main course about £14.75. 3-courses about £26.
Pk lunch: £7.50.
Route: 300m.
017684 83635
info@troutbeckinn.co.uk
thetroutbeckinn.co.uk

Lane Head Farm Country Guest House
Troutbeck, Nr. Keswick, Cumbria, CA11 0SY
Run by: Mandy Aldom & Pawel Stolarczyk

A warm welcome to C2C from the new couple running Lane Head. Bang on the route, much money has been spent restoring this lovely old farmhouse. There is now a bar and evening meals are provided so long as you give a couple of days notice. There is a drying room and 7 en-suite rooms (two with baths and showers over), each sleeping 2 people. Great place to relax after a hard days cycling. Hosepipe to wash down bikes.
Rooms: 1T, 4D, 2 4-posters.
B&B: from £35-£40.
Eve meal: £15 for 2 courses; £20 for 3. Please book in advance.
Pk lunch: please pre-order.
4-star Guest Accommodation.
Free wifi. Drying facilities. Secure storage.

017687 79220
info@laneheadfarm.co.uk
laneheadfarm.co.uk

MOTHERBY & PENRUDDOCK

ACCOMMODATION

Motherby House, Motherby, nr Penrith, Cumbria CA11 0RJ

Run by: Jacquie Freeborn

Warm, friendly former 18th century farmhouse. Excellent food for outdoor appetites and muddy clothes welcome. Jacquie can take groups of up to 12. There is no supplementary charge for single occupancy. Rooms are flexible so a family room can also be used as a twin or double.

Rooms: 2F. Plus singles, doubles and twins.
B&B: £34.50.
Eve meal: £19.50 for 3 courses.
Pk lunch: £6.50.
Nearest pub: 1.5km.
017684 83368
jacquie@motherbyhouse.co.uk
motherbyhouse.co.uk

Herdwick Inn, Penruddock, Cumbria, CA11 0QU

Run by: Simon Brown

Lovely old 18th century coaching inn rescued from neglect late last year by Simon Brown, who also owns the Punchbowl in Askham. The Herdwick once again welcomes cyclists. Good use of local produce in the restaurant and fine Jennings ales in the cosy bar.

B&B: from £30 (£40 at weekends).
Rooms: 2T, 2D.
Eve meal: £8 to £13 for main courses.
Around £20 for 3-courses.
Pk Lunch: please pre-order.
Secure lock-up.
017684 83007
info@herdwickinn.com
herdwickinn.com

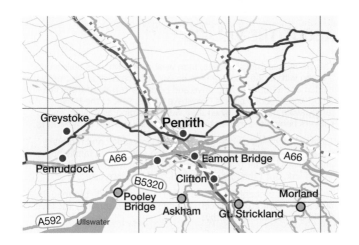

WIGGO'S WAY

PENRUDDOCK → STANHOPE

Via Appleby, Brough and Middleton-in-Teesdale

Penruddock to Great Strickland: 12.6 miles

The first section of Wiggo's Way (Penruddock to Gt Strickland) was added in 2011 and called the Yellow Jersey Loop, to allow you to get to Penrith via Ullswater, taking in such picturesque villages as Askham. For 2014, this route was extended from Great Strickland, visited by Sir Bradley and Team Sky in 2012, to take in a tour through the middle Eden Valley to Appleby and then to Brough, finishing by crossing the Pennines to Middleton in Teesdale and rejoining the C2C at Stanhope.

The first section takes you through the Lowther Estate with its fine castle. There are also places along here perfect for an overnight stay. Askham is one of the prettiest villages in Cumbria, and Great Strickland is also worth a stop. To get back on the C2C you simply pick up a section of the Pennine Cycleway which takes you to the eastern fringes of Penrith, from where you head up to Beacon Fell from Carletonhill. Or you simply continue along the fabulous new braid to Stanhope, via Teesdale.

To see the rest of Wiggo's Way and get all the route details and places to stop, please see page 110 →

GREYSTOKE

ABOUT THE VILLAGE

This traditional English village, 8km west of Penrith, was built around a green with a pub and a church the size of a cathedral. Discreetly hidden at the top of a long drive and behind a curtain of trees in a 3,000-acre wooded park is Greystoke Castle, seat of the Howard family since the 1500s when they were emerging as movers and shakers behind the monarchies of the late Tudors and early Stuarts.

Tarzan is modelled on one former Baron Greystoke, and there are certainly enough trees for any Lord of the Apes. It is a family home and business rather than a theme park, so not much is made of the Tarzan link, but I thought Tarzan fans might be interested.

The village is probably Roman in origin, lying alongside the road they built from Penrith to Troutbeck. The name means 'place by the River Creik', a small stream nearby.

Though most of the village dates from the 17th century, the foundation of the Perpendicular-style church was laid in the mid-1200s, though building did not start until 1382 and went on into the next century. The bells that still ring out date from the Middle Ages as does some of the wonderful stained glass.

The Spillers Stone in the village was thought to be a plague stone, where plague victims left coins in a pool of vinegar on its concave surface. The vinegar was supposed to protect the healthy, who left food there for sufferers.

Greystoke Castle, originally constructed in 1129, was an integral part of village life. It was built as protection against Scottish Border raiders - Reivers - as they were known. Reiving, a mixture of thieving, murdering and blackmailing, came to dominate the area.

As if that were not enough, then came Cromwell who destroyed much of Greystoke during the Civil War. In 1868 a devastating fire ensured that only the medieval pele (fortified) tower of the castle and a few Georgian interiors survived. The present building, though Elizabethan in style, actually dates from the 19th century.

The nearby countryside boasts a number of fine old fortified houses complete with pele towers, notably Blencowe Hall, Greenthwaite Hall, and Johnby Hall. All are reminders of these bloody times.

The Boot and Shoe pub in the village acquired its name because of the strange sartorial habit of a former Duke of Norfolk of wearing a shoe on one foot and a boot on the other, to ease the pain of crippling gout. Whether or not he shuffled down the long drive and across the green to the pub is not recorded.

The village is also home to Greystoke Stables, a successful racehorse training yard. Notable victories include Lucius (1978) and Hallo Dandy (1982) in the Grand National and three successes in the King George VI Chase, the feature race of Kempton Park's Boxing Day meeting.

ACCOMMODATION

Brathen, The Thorpe, Greystoke, nr Penrith, Cumbria CA11 0TJ

Run by: Christine Mole

Comfortable barn conversion on the outskirts of the village with a warm welcome and hearty breakfasts using local produce. Secure storage plus washing and drying facilities.

Rooms: 2D, 2T, 2F.
B&B: £38 (en-suite)
Pk lunch: £4.50.
On route.
Pub 300 yds.
017684 83595
stay@brathen.co.uk
brathen.co.uk

Beech House, Berrier Rd, Greystoke CA11 0UE

Run by: Jill McAlea

Grade II listed 17th century smallholding with pigs and hens, neighbouring Greystoke castle and only 100 metres from the Boot & Shoe. Beech House is part of Lattendales country house, and is a splendid spot. All rooms have tea and coffee making facilities, TV and wifi.

Rooms: 1D, 2F (3 and 4 beds in each).
B&B: £40. Single occ £50-£60.
Pk lunch: by arrangement.
Secure cycle storage.
017684 80829 \ 07899 794698
jillmcalea@talk21.com
beechhousegreystoke.co.uk

Boot & Shoe, Greystoke, Penrith, CA11 0TP

Run by: Jan & Ben Mandale

The Boot & Shoe is one of the great success stories of the C2C since Jan and Ben took the reins eight years ago. There's a real buzz about the place; cyclists, visitors and locals jostle for place while Jan hands out steaming plates of excellent food, ranging from chicken balti to local dishes like lamb Henry. A real community hub. Log fire in the bar, stove in the lounge, plus selection of well kept real ales. Evening meals and bar meals served in the restaurant, bar or outside in the beer garden or on the patio.

Rooms: 4T+1D/T (en-suite).
B&B: £44 to £55 (single occ).
Eve meal: £5.95-£12.95 (main courses).
Secure lock-up cycle shed.
017684 83343
mandale@lineone.net
boot-and-shoe.com

🍴 WHERE TO EAT

Greystoke Cycle Café, CA11 0UT. A charming 'cycle barn' where cakes and other home-made goodies are available, rain or shine. Self-service tea, flapjacks between 10-6. Chain oil, free bottle refills, spare inner tubes and more. If you are a large group, please book.
017684 83984
annie@greystokecyclecafe.co.uk
greystokecyclecafe.co.uk

NEWTON REIGNY

Newton Reigny lies within the ancient forest of Inglewood which was once one of the largest hunting grounds in the country. The village derives its name from the family of De Reigny who had the manor during the the reign of Henry II and held it by the practice of 'offering' horsemen to serve against Scotland. The manor of Newton is now part of the possessions of the Earl of Lonsdale, whose ancestor Hugh de Lowther obtained it in 1290.

🍴 WHERE TO EAT

Sun Inn, Newton Reigny, Penrith CA11 0AP
Run by: Lucy Jakeman
The Jakeman family took over in 2015 and are breathing life back into this popular 17th century coaching inn. It is located in a picturesque village bang on the route, just before Penrith. Warm and welcoming atmosphere. Good traditional cask ales, great dining facilities, excellent home cooked food. Accommodation will be back on tap towards the end of the season, in time for the spring start to 2016. Meals served lunch and dinner, plus afternoon tea, cakes and coffee.
01768 867055
thesuninnnewtonreigny14@gmail.com
thesuninnnr.co.uk

ASKHAM

🍴 WHERE TO EAT

Abbott Lodge tea room and ice cream makers, Clifton, Nr Penrith, Cumbria, CA10 2HD.
Steven and Claire Bland run a working dairy farm making more than 40 flavours of top quality homemade Jersey ice cream.
Open 11am – 5pm daily. Children's area and meet-the-cows facility.
01931 712720
abbottlodgejerseyicecream.co.uk

Askham Hall Kitchen Garden Cafe, Askham, Penrith CA10 2PF
Run by: Charles Lowther

Wonderful stop-off on the new Wiggo's Way braid via Ullswater braid. Handy for Clifton and Penrith. Café and gardens open to the public in the grounds of Askham Hall – an elegant Grade I listed building which has recently been converted into a restaurant and hotel with private spa and outdoor pool in one of the most delightful villages in Cumbria. Coffees, cakes and light lunches available as is beer and wine. During the spring summer months (peak times) you can enjoy pizzas from the outdoor wood-fired oven and homemade ice-creams. Askham Hall is also home to rare breed animals which can be seen as part of the garden tour. Same owner as the estimable George and Dragon in nearby Clifton.

Open every day except Saturdays until October half-term, 10am – 5pm, then Friday – Sunday, 11am – 4pm for the rest of the year except for a close period in January and early February.

01931 712350
enquiries@askhamhall.co.uk
askhamhall.co.uk

ACCOMMODATION

Askham Hall, Askham, Penrith CA10 2PF
Run by: Charles Lowther

Now open with a restaurant spread through three rooms, 12 bedrooms (15 from 2016) with a spa and outdoor heated pool, gardens and café open to the public and a converted party barn. Its style? A luxurious, intimate, unpretentious home from home which is up-to-date, full of charm and somewhere you can relax after a hard day's cycling. This is a foodlover's haven: chef Richard Swale worked for Michelin 3-star Marc Veyrat in Annecy, France and John Burton Race in London. He also did a stint at NOMA, the world's top-rated restaurant. Beef and pork are home raised and herbs and veg are grown in the gardens. Staying here is like being a house guest at a country home. Flawless. Now in the Good Hotel Guide.

Rooms: 12.
B&B: from £75 per person (sharing).
Eve meal: 3-courses plus nibbles £50.
Tasting menu £65.
Exemplary wine list.
Secure lock-up and drying facilities.

01931 712350
enquiries@askhamhall.co.uk
askhamhall.co.uk

Punchbowl Inn, Askham, Penrith CA10 2PF
Run by: Simon Brown

Splendid old coaching inn in one of the most scenic places along the route. This is a big place with lots of rooms and a great selection of beers plus a bustling business in upmarket but reasonably priced pub food. With six rooms, the Punchbowl is ideal for small groups, and has free wifi as well as a secure storage area for bikes.

Rooms: 6T/D.
B&B: from £45.
Eve meal: around £20 for 3-courses.
Mains around £10.
Pk lunch: pse pre-order.
Secure lock-up.
Freeview flatscreens, free wifi.
01931 712443
punchbowlinnaskham@gmail.com
punchbowlinnaskham.com

PENRITH

▶ DIRECTIONS

Leaving Greystoke, then on to Newton Reigny and Penrith

- You soon pass Blencow Hall. It is a beautifully restored building just before you get to the village of Little Blencow. Just up the road follow signs to the right and you will enter Penrith via Newton Reigny and Newton Rigg.
- On leaving Newton Rigg campus go underneath the M6 and turn right at the T-junction, going into town along Robinson Street, across Scotland Rd and into Drover's Lane.
  The route is well sign-posted.
- You know you are on the right tracks when you find yourself exiting Penrith up Fell Lane – a steep climb to a T-junction at the top.

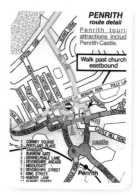

ABOUT THE TOWN

A handsome red sandstone market town, Penrith was the capital of the Kingdom of Cumbria in the 9th and 10th centuries, a time when the area was allied to Scotland as a semi-independent part of the Kingdom of Strathclyde. Since it was on the main north-south road it also witnessed more than its fair share of bloody action during border conflicts; the Scots put the town to torch three times during the 14th century alone.

Its early growth was restricted because the town had no water supply, but in 1385 Bishop Strickland diverted Thacka Beck from the river Peterill, an eco-sensitive agreement that allowed the townspeople to draw only as much water daily from the Petterill as would flow through the eye of a millstone (still on view outside the Tourist Information Centre).

By the 18th century it was an important cattle market. The oldest streets in the town, Burrowgate and Sandgate, are narrow, unspoilt and 800 years old. Two traditional shops have also survived, as if preserved in aspic: Graham's, Penrith's answer to Fortnum & Mason; and Arnisons, the drapers, established in 1740 in the building that was once the home of Wordsworth's grandparents. The poet and his sister Dorothy attended the Dame Anne Birkett School, overlooking St Andrew's Churchyard and final resting place of Owen Caesarius, a legendary giant and King of All Cumbria.

They are far from the only famous figures from history associated with the town. As 'Guardian of the West March towards Scotland', the Duke of Gloucester plotted his way towards being crowned Richard III from behind the sandstone ramparts of the magnificent Penrith Castle.

It was not all skulduggery though: he also stayed at one of the pubs in town and is even said to have had a private underground passage to it so that he could go back and forth unseen. The link is commemorated in the pub's name, the Gloucester Arms, and some of the original stonework is still there – which is scarcely true of the castle which was a ruin by the mid 16th century, donating much of its stonework to the town's buildings.

The George Hotel provided lodgings for Bonnie Prince Charlie in 1745, during his ill-fated foray south in search of the crown.

Others linked to Penrith include Mary Queen of Scots, Oliver Cromwell and the writer, Anthony Trollope. The first must have spent most of her life on horseback to get to all the places she is alleged to have visited, though in the case of Penrith the connection is justified. Cromwell occupied the town in 1654 and though the pen is mightier than the sword, Trollope is not thought to have caused as much bloodshed. More recently, the area was immortalised in Bruce Robinson's classic film comedy of 1987, 'Withnail and I', in which the area is again traumatised – this time by a pair of drunken wannabe actors.

Above Penrith is Beacon Hill, past which you will shortly be cycling. Beacons have been lit there through the ages to warn of threat of invasion. Its views are stunning.

PLACES OF INTEREST

Penrith Museum and Tourist Information Centre
Housed in the former Robinson's School, an Elizabethan building altered in 1670 and a school until the early 1970s. The museum covers the history, geology and archaeology of the Penrith area. Free entry.
01768 867466

St Andrew's Church
The Giant's Grave in the Churchyard is that of Owen Caesarius, the legendary slayer of monsters from Inglewood Forest. The tower is 12th century, the rest dates from 1720, being rebuilt after a fire. The stained-glass windows were added in 1870.

Wordsworth Bookshop,
St Andrew's Churchyard
01768 210604

The town's architecture .
Take a walk around. Well worth a stopover.

Penrith Castle
Started in 1399, once home to Richard III but abandoned after his death. Free entry.

Booths
Brunswick Road.
Wonderfully stocked supermarket with cafe and takeaway.

🍴 WHERE TO EAT

BEWICKS COFFEE SHOP & BISTRO, Princes Court. Accomplished and simple; lovely setting, reasonable prices: 01768 864764

FOUR & TWENTY, 42 King St. Cutting edge Anglo-French style cooking by chefs with background: three of them cut their teeth in Michelin-starred kitchens. A way overdue addition to the town's culinary action. 01768 210231. info@fourandtwentypenrith.co.uk. fourandtwentypenrith.co.uk.

GEORGE HOTEL, Devonshire St. Does everything from lounge snacks to formal restaurant. Reliable and reasonable: 01768 862696.

MOO BAR, 52 King St. A new and much needed addition to the Penrith scene: a craft beer bar with lots of choice. 01768 606637.

THE NARROWBAR CAFÉ, 13 Devonshire St. Splendid little café bar offering Lavazza coffee, milkshakes and a range of hot, soft and alcoholic drinks. Snacks and sweet treats served until 5pm, breakfasts and lunches up until 4pm. Home cooked daily changing specials, such as beef and barley stew, chorizo and pepper risotto, spicy lamb kofta wraps, homity pie and their famous fishcakes. Run by Phil and Penny Wood. 01768 891417.

ABBOTT LODGE TEA ROOM and ice cream makers, Clifton, Nr Penrith, Cumbria, CA10 2HD. 01931 712720. Steven and Claire Bland run a working dairy farm making more than 40 flavours of top quality homemade Jersey ice cream. Open 11am - 5pm daily. Children's area and see-the-cows facility. abbottlodgejerseyicecream.co.uk.

FLYING BACON, 3 Middlegate, Penrith, CA11 7PG. Right in the centre of town, this new café and gallery offers lots of home-baked treats plus heartier fare. Bacon butties only £2.50 and the cakes are worth a detour. Coffee specialists, this is a relaxing place to stop off. You can even take your bike and a bottle of wine inside (corkage for the wine). **Open seven days a week 9-5.** 01768 867339 rje1234@hotmail.co.uk | flyingbacon.co.uk

CYCLE SHOPS

Arragons, Brunswick Road.
01768 890 344
arragonscycles.com

Harpers Cycles, 1-2 Middlegate
01768 864 475

ACCOMMODATION

The George and Dragon, Clifton, nr Penrith, Cumbria CA10 2ER
Run by: Charles Lowther

Ideal for groups who fancy a night of affordable comfort, the George and Dragon hits all the right notes: top quality food (Michelin and Good Food Guide recommended), beautifully refurbished and comfortable rooms, fine ales in a welcoming bar and a great wine list. Secure lock up for bikes (they welcome cyclists). The George and Dragon is a Georgian gem run by Charles Lowther, whose family has been in the area for 800 years. Clifton is on the A6, just a couple of miles from the centre of town, or accessible by back lanes via Brougham. It's almost bang on the new Ullswater braid. Courtyard and garden plus free wifi. Food is locally sourced and worth a trip for this alone.

Rooms: 7D (all with king size beds), 2T, 2F.
B&B: from £47.50pp sharing. £85 single occ.
Eve meal: mains from £13.50. 3-courses from £25.
Pk lunch: on request.
Bar open all day serving tea, coffee and snacks.
Lunch: 12-2.30.
Dinner: 6-9pm.
01768 865381
enquiries@georgeanddragonclifton.co.uk
georgeanddragonclifton.co.uk

Strickland Arms, Great Strickland, Penrith, CA10 3DF
Run by: Anton & Penny Flaherty

WILL ORGANISE YOUR TRIP FOR YOU. Famously playing host to Wiggo and Team Sky during the 2012 Tour of Britain, the Arms is going from strength to strength. The new fleece-lined log-built yurt sleeps 10 and there's room for 6 more in the pub. The Arms is on the new C2C route via Ullswater, details of which can be found on the C2C website's Home Page map browser. It's a warm and friendly pub with lots of character, in the heart of Eden Valley, five miles from Penrith. The pub now has Wiggo's yellow jersey from the Tour de France, plus other Team Sky mementos. Real fires, cask ales, a decent selection of wines to go with homemade food cooked by Penny.

Rooms: 2T/D.
Yurt: 10s from £25.
B&B: £30-£45.
Eve meal: £6 - £15.
Pk lunch: Yes - depends what you want.
Secure lock up. Bike washing facility.
01931 712238
stricklandarmspenrith@hotmail.co.uk
thestricklandarms.co.uk

North Lakes Hotel and Spa, Ullswater Road, Penrith, CA11 8QT
Run by: Duty Manager

The 84 bedroomed 4 star North Lakes Hotel and Spa is the perfect place to replenish your energy levels after a hard day's slog with great food, comfortable beds and a well-equipped spa complete with steam room and sauna including massages from our trained therapists. After a good night's sleep the hotel's renowned and hearty breakfast will set you up right for the day ahead.

B&B: from £57.45 (2 sharing a twin room).
Rooms: 84 T/D/S plus suites.
Eve meal: restaurant and bar.
2-course £16.95, 3-courses £19.95.
Secure cycle storage and drying facilities.
01768 868111
nlakes@shirehotels.com
shirehotels.co.uk/our-hotels/north-lakes/

Wayfarers Hostel, 19 Brunswick Sq, Penrith, CA11 7LR

Run by: Mark Rhodes

Great addition to Penrith, at last somewhere that can take large groups at the most popular stop-off. The route passes 50m from the doorstep, Wayfarers is geared up for cyclists. It has secure indoor bike storage, a drying room, and cleaning and maintenance facilities. Can accommodate up to 16, in comfort. Newly refurbished, there's a lounge, full kitchen and dining facilities and an outside seating area. All rooms are en-suite with made up beds (sheets & duvets), lockers, bedside lights, towels for hire (£1) and free WiFi. Individuals, small parties and groups of up to 18 are welcome.

Rooms: 1T, 2X4 berth, 1X6-berth.
B&B: £22.
B'fast: £4 (continental).
Pk lunch: £5.
Secure lock-up. Drying room.
Cleaning facilities.
01768 866011
guests@wayfarershostel.com
wayfarershostel.com

....

Tynedale Guest House, 4 Victoria Road, Penrith, CA11 8HR

Run by: Marguerite & Thomas Powley

Happy to handle large groups. High level of comfort and attention to detail, and long experience of looking after C2Cers. Quality accommodation in a warm and friendly environment offering a delicious, locally sourced English breakfast. Stone built and highly secure cycle storage, plus free wifi. An excellent pedal-stop for weary C2Cers. Pubs and restaurants all close by. 'Home baked treats to go, usually sticky flapjack,' says Marguerite. A truly warm welcome!.

Rooms: 1S, 2T,4D,3F.
B&B: from £34.
Eve meal: pubs and restaurants are nearby.
Pk lunch: please pre-order.
Secure cycle parking.
Distance from route: 300 metres.
Pub: 200 metres
01768 867491
marguerite@tynedaleguesthouse.wanadoo.co.uk
tynedale-guesthouse.co.uk

The Crown Hotel, Eamont Bridge, Penrith CA10 2BX

Run by: Anna & Mike

This 17th century former coaching inn is less than a mile from the centre of Penrith, on the A6 southbound. The Crown has 14 bedrooms so is ideal for groups. There's a lock up for bikes and a big bar and eating area. Dinner is reasonably priced. Can take groups of up to 12. Now a vibrant hub of the local community, runs a beer festival and is the new home of Penrith Chess Club.

Rooms: 14 T/D/S/F - half en-suite.
Bed: from £35-£40
(Family room is £75 to £100 depending on whether it's for 3 or 4 people).
B'fast: £5. **Eve meal:** from £8.
Pk lunch: £5.
01768 892092 / 07982 124569
mikegardener56@yahoo.com
thecrown-hotel.co.uk

Blue Swallow Guest House, 11 Victoria Road, Penrith, CA11 8HR

Run by: Peter and Cynthia Barry

Clean, comfortable rooms, six of which are en-suite and one has a private bathroom. Good for groups of up to 24. Free wifi plus tv and dvds, Tea/Coffee trays. Excellent English breakfast using local produce. Secure lock up for cycles. Easy access to eating and drinking establishments. Well recommended with lots of repeat business.

Rooms: 4D, 4T, 2S, 3F (6 en-suite, one with private facilities).
B&B: £37-£50. (single occ: £42 & £48)
Open all year.
Eve meal: surrounded by pubs and restaurants.
Pk lunch: £7- pre-ordered please. 300m from route.
Pubs: 50m. **Visit England:** 4-star.
01768 866335
info@blueswallow.co.uk
blueswallow.co.uk

Caledonia Guest House, 8 Victoria Road, Penrith, CA11 8HR

Run by: Ian & Sue Rhind

A comfortable friendly guest house close to the C2C route and the town centre, handy for bars and restaurants. All rooms are en-suite and have flat screen TVs with freeview, tea and coffee making facilities and hair driers. An excellent full English Breakfast will set you up for your next day's ride. There is secure storage for bikes in the bike shed. All major debit and credit cards accepted.

Rooms: 2D, 3T, 1F.
B&B: £36-£50.
Pk lunch: £6.
Pub: 200m.
VisitBritain: 4-star.
Secure bike shed. Free wifi.
01768 864482
ian.rhind1@virgin.net
caledoniaguesthouse.co.uk

@Eden Gate, 5 Victoria Road, Penrith, CA11 8HR
Run by: Lorraine & Roger Roberts

A family run Victorian guest house offering welcoming accommodation 250m from Penrith's many town centre pubs and restaurants. All the rooms now have freeview TV, DAB radios/iPod docks and free wi-fi. There is secure storage and washing facilities for cycles and the owners are happy to dry wet gear. They can also accommodate up to 12 and are happy to coordinate accommodation for larger groups. For support vehicles there is private off-street parking. Mid-week deals now available.

Rooms: 1D, 1T, 1D/T, 2F
(can sleep 3 in separate beds).
4 en-suite, 1 with private facilities.
B&B: from £36.
Pk lunch: £7 (please pre-order).
Pub: 250m.

Drying facilities and secure lock-up.
VisitEngland: 4-star and Cyclists Welcome.
01768 866538
enquire@edengateguesthouse.co.uk
edengateguesthouse.co.uk

George Hotel, Devonshire St, Penrith, Cumbria CA11 7SU
Run by: Lake District Hotels

A great landmark in the centre of town, the George has for many generations been the place to meet. Stylish and spacious, this old world hotel with modern twists has much to offer C2Cers. As well as secure lock-ups for bikes, there are comfortable rooms plus a good spread of locally sourced dishes on both the restaurant and bar menus. Ideal for groups as there are 35 rooms. Famous for afternoon teas.

Rooms: 29 D/T, 6S.
B&B: from £45.
Eve meal: from £10 to around
£27 for a 3-course à la carte meal.
Lunch: similar. **Afternoon tea:** from £15.95.
Secure lock up. Drying facilities.
01768 862696
georgehotel@lakedistricthotels.net
lakedistricthotels.net/georgehotel

Foundry 34, 34 Burrowgate, Penrith, CA4 7TA
Run by: Daniel Harding

Smart new 'boutique' hotel, restaurant and bar in the centre of town. Geared up for cycling, Foundry 34 is also keen on food, and serves up some great local produce, specialising in steaks. There's also a decent wine list and a cocktail bar. Groovy new addition to Penrith.

Rooms: 2S, 3T/D, 2D.
B&B: from £40.
Eve meal: yes - from £9 to £20.
Pk lunch: yes.

Cycle storage and drying facilities.
01768 210099
bookings@foundry-34.co.uk
foundry-34.co.uk

The New Vic, 46 Castlegate, Penrith, CA11 7HY

Run by: Debbie Creighton

Originally a 17th century coaching inn, the New Vic offers cheap rooms and drink and great service. Bikes are securely stored in the old ice house. This is a friendly, no-nonsense local boozer and the emphasis is on quality ale and lively atmosphere.

Rooms: 6 S/D/T - the rooms are flexible. All en-suite.

B&B: £30.

01768 862467

mojo1966@hotmail.co.uk

LANGWATHBY

▶ DIRECTIONS

Last chance to take it easy before the serious stuff starts

- You leave Penrith along Fell Lane before turning right onto Beacon Edge. There are fabulous views from here followed by a long descent to the B6412. Enjoy it while you can; the really serious bit is about to start.

- Around Langwathby are the villages of Great Salkeld, Edenhall and Little Salkeld. If you are overnighting at Great Salkeld (the food at the Highland Drove is exceptional and has been featured in the Michelin good pub food guide) then take a left along the B6412 for 3km. Great Salkeld is a pretty little village and the pub does B&B.

- If you turn right onto the B6412 you are soon in the village of Edenhall, where the Eden Hall Country House offers splendid accommodation and good food. Both villages are close to Langwathby, with its lovely village green and pub. At Little Salkeld the Atkinson family run an equine centre with accommodation.

- There's a railway station that services the popular Carlisle to Settle line. This area is popular for overnight stops because the surrounding villages are well-placed for attacking Hartside and the other hills that make the next section the hardest.

- Melmerby, on the A686 about 5km from Langwathby, is also popular. There's a pub there, a famous bakery, and now some spectacular places to stay.

- Langwathby was a Viking settlement; Edenhall once boasted a fine stately home; and Little Salkeld has its watermill. They are all close to the Long Meg and Little Meg stone circles.

- Long Meg comprises a megalith at the head of 60 stones. The whole monument is some 360ft (115m) in diameter and is well worth a stop.

ACCOMMODATION

The Highland Drove Inn & Kyloes Restaurant, Great Salkeld, Langwathby, Penrith, CA11 9NA

Run by: Donald & Christine Newton

Ideal for groups of up to 12, this real country pub has open fires, real ale, quality wines and a beer garden. Good range of bar food with separate 'Kyloes' restaurant serving eclectic and award winning cuisine. Winner of Cumbria Dining Pub of the Year plus CAMRA's Real Ale Pub of the Year. Also in the Michelin 'inns with restaurants' guide. Top spot with well chosen wine list with a new pub, the Cross Keys, recently opened on the edge of Penrith on the A686 near the rugby ground. Marginal price rises driven by VAT. Not open during the afternoon.

Rooms: 4D/T & 1F.
B&B: £37.50. Single occ. £42.50.
Eve meal: Bar: 2-courses from £12.
Restaurant 2-courses £18-£20.
Pk lunch: £7.50.
On alternative route via Kirkoswald.
Distance from route: 3km - but worth every inch.
01768 898349 \ 07720 347822
highlanddrove@kyloes.co.uk
kyloes.co.uk

....

North Dyke Farm,

Run by: Philip and Liz Horn

Just over a mile from the Highland Drove Inn, where you can eat and drink, North Dyke Farm commands great views of the Fells with 5 pitches plus a static caravan for rent. Reviews are excellent, despite being on a slightly sloping field. There are hook-ups available. The amenities block is in an adjoing field and is small but comfortable with one toilet and shower for each sex. There's an additional (outdoor, but secluded) urinal in the corner of the main field. There are also washing up and laundry facilities

£10 per pitch. Certified Site.
Member of the Camping and Caravan Club.
01768 898349 / 07720 347822
ukcampsite.co.uk

CYCLISTS WELCOME
WELCOME CYCLISTS

Eden Hall Country Hotel & Restaurant, Edenhall
Langwathby, CA11 8SX

Run by: Paula & Wayne Williams

Now includes a brand new luxury budget price apartment for 6. Eden Hall is 2.5 miles outside Penrith and a mile short of Langwathby, this is a smart country house hotel in beautiful surroundings. Bar meals and restaurant meals available. Can be eaten in dining room or bar. Prices range from £5.95 for a bar meal to £15.95. Free view flat screen digital TV, wifi throughout, telephone, tea/coffee in all rooms. Secure cycle storage and drying facilities. Email or call for a brochure. Apartment has kitchen with washer/dryer. Sky HD TV.

Rooms: 3S, 11D, 5T (en-suite).
B&B: £37.50-£55.
Apartment: sleeps 6 in 3T rooms - £149 (no b'fast).
Eve meal: from £5.95 to £15.95.
Pk lunch: £5.95 (extensive and filling).
VisitBritain: 2-star hotel.
01768 881454
info@edenhallhotel.co.uk
edenhallhotel.co.uk

Bank House Farm, Little Salkeld, Langwathby, Penrith CA10 1NN

Run by: Nancy & Ray Atkinson

Bank House Farm is situated in the delightful village of Little Salkeld on the main route at the bottom of the big climbs, just before Hartside pass. Static caravan accommodation that can be used for B&B or self catering. The caravans are spacious and perfect for individuals, families and large groups up to 32. Camping is available in the orchard with the shower block close by containing free showers, toilet and pot washing facilities, all under one roof. Secure cycle storage. Food can be bought from the nearby pub at Langwathby and the village also has a shop and off-licence. Bank House can provide transport for you and your bikes so could be an ideal base for the whole trip. Cold drinks and snack machines on site, and lift to the pub 1.5 miles away offered.

B&B: £35.
Self-catering: from £25.
Camping: £10pp.
B'fast for campers: £10 or £5 for bacon butty and cup of tea.
Eve meal: local pubs.
Pk lunches: £5.
Secure cycle storage & wash down facilities. On route.
Pub: 1.2 miles.
01768 881257 / 07878 536892
bankhouseequ@aol.com
c2c-cycle-accommodation.co.uk

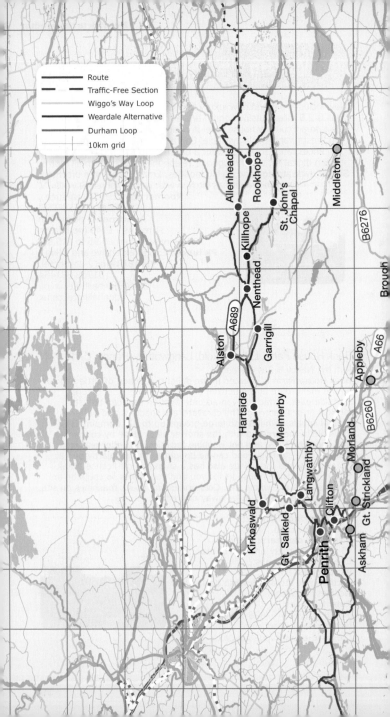

LANGWATHBY → ALLENHEADS

28 miles (0 miles traffic-free)

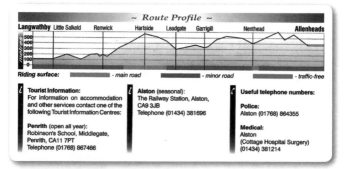

~ Route Profile ~

Tourist Information:
For information on accommodation and other services contact one of the following Tourist Information Centres:

Penrith (open all year):
Robinson's School, Middlegate, Penrith, CA11 7PT
Telephone (01768) 867466

Alston (seasonal):
The Railway Station, Alston, CA9 3JB
Telephone (01434) 381696

Useful telephone numbers:

Police:
Alston (01768) 864355

Medical:
Alston
(Cottage Hospital Surgery)
(01434) 381214

KIRKOSWALD & LAZONBY

▶ DIRECTIONS

To divert to Eden or not to divert to Eden. That is the question

- Athough not on the official C2C route, the neighbouring villages of Kirkoswald and Lazonby see a fair amount of cycle traffic opting to follow the Eden Valley. When you exit Langwathby you will be presented with choices about what route to take.
- But if you want to go directly to Kirkoswald you should go left at milemarker 57, just before Langwathby, and head through Great Salkeld, Lazonby and over the River Eden.
- Other options take you into Langwathby, from where you head north towards Little Salkeld and Glassonby.
- If you are taking this alternative detour to Kirkoswald, leave the main C2C route at milemarker 61.5, head through Glassonby and down the hill into Kirkoswald. Make your way back to the route proper via Viol Moor running parallel to the Raven Beck and onto Four Lane End at milemarker 64.2.
- If you decide to forgo the joys of Kirkoswald, just plough straight up the main route and you are soon at Four Lane End.

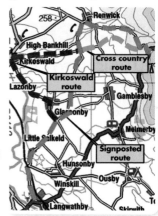

- At Four Lane End you can turn right onto the cross-country route over Hartside, but if you do, be warned, you will be pushing or carrying your bike for a lot of the stretch.
- The alternative takes you to Renwick, a winding and steep ascent (I suspect I am not the only cyclist to have hopped out of the saddle for a rest a couple of times).

 ## FOOD & DRINK

Fetherston Arms, Kirkoswald CA10 1DQ
Run by: brothers Alan & Michael Collinson
A busy country pub situated on the lovely village square of Kirkoswald. Popular with locals and visitors alike, renowned in the area for its quality home-cooked food and great selection of well kept real ales. Great place to sample one of the home-made pies and enjoy a pint of local beer. Open every evening and all day at weekends. Solway Camra Pub of the Year (2014).
01768 898284
alancollinson@yahoo.com

CAMPING & SWIMMING

Open air swimming: there's a wonderful lido and campsite (on the banks of the Eden) at Lazonby, just off the B6413, just beyond the village. 07905 076001.
lazonbypool.co.uk.

Campsite enquiries, contact David Ousby at the Midland Hotel in Lazonby on 01768 898901. Prices: Per pitch including showers (tent/caravan/campervan): £15.

MELMERBY & RENWICK

WHERE TO EAT

The Shepherds Inn – Lovely country pub next to the village shop. Under new ownership and undergoing serious change at time of going to press. This has been - and will soon be again - a very fine hostelry serving excellent food. The pub was bought earlier this year and the new owners have been busy about their renovation work. The climb up to Hartside from Melmerby is all on road and offers stunning views as well as a challenging, uphill cycle ride all the way to the cafe at Hartside summit. Be aware though that this section of road can get quite busy.
01768 880866

ACCOMMODATION

The Old Village Bakery, Melmerby, Penrith, Cumbria, CA10 1HE
Run by: Michael & his team
Excellent new resource on the route, taken over last summer by Michael and Paul and their small team. Paul bakes the breads and cakes in the old kitchen and the team make the jams and chutneys. The shop does cakeaways, there's fresh home-made soup, home-baked quiche every day, plus pies and full lunches as well as paninis, sandwiches, lemon drizzle cakes, a Bakery burger plus a hearty breakfast. It's organic, it's home made - it's the Melmerby Bakery as it originally was.
Opening hours: Mon-Thurs: 9.30-4.30; Fri-Sat 9-5; Sun 9.30-5.
01768 881811
info@village-bakery.com
village-bakery.com

Gate House Bed and Breakfast, Melmerby, Penrith, CA10 1HF
Run by: Ann Black
A warm welcome awaits as does a delicious and nutritious breakfast at this period sandstone detached house. As locations go along the C2C, this is hard to beat: at the foot of Hartside, you get the biggest climb out of the way first thing. Gate House has two rooms, one double room with en-suite shower, one twin room with private facilities. A further single room is also available upon request. The very fine local pub, which serves evening meals, is just 200 metres away. Ann and Danny are wonderful hosts and Danny works on the C2C so knows it back to front.
Rooms: 1T, 1D.
B&B: from £30 (rooms £60 for T and £70 for D).
Single occ. £40.
Eve meal: local pub.
Pk lunch: yes.
Secure lock-up.
Pub: 200m.
01768 889126
dannyann@hotmail.co.uk
gatehousebandb.co.uk

Addingham View, Gamblesby, Penrith, Cumbria, CA10 1JA
Run by: Simon & Kirsty Cogan
An ideal place to stop before the assault on Hartside, located just
under 2 miles from the C2C route (mostly downhill). Addingham View
is an 1860s sandstone home, situated in the tranquil farming village
of Gamblesby. You can be sure of a warm welcome from Simon and
Kirsty after a hard day's cycling, with home made cake on arrival. All
guest rooms are fully en-suite and have recently been redecorated.
The dining table can be set for you if you would like to bring your
evening meal, or alternatively lifts to the pub are available if you
prefer to eat out.
Rooms: 3D or 2T & 1D.
B&B: £37.50-£42.50 per person (rooms
£75 - £85 each). Discount available for
single occupancy.

Eve meal: information given on variety of
local pubs. Free transport provided to and
from same.
Secure, locked cycle storage.
Bike cleaning facilities. Free Wi-Fi.
01768 889254 / 07872 934437
addinghamview@gmail.com
addinghamviewbandb.co.uk

ALSTON

▶ DIRECTIONS

Up Hartside, and back down again

- Whichever way you go, it is a hard climb from Little Salkeld but at
  the top awaits Hartside Café, a (motor)bikers' haven. At 580 metres
  (1900 feet), it is the highest tea shop in England and on a fine day
  you can see across the Solway Firth to Scotland. The views of the
  Eden Valley are terrific: not for nothing was the drive along the A686
  voted one of the ten best in the world by the AA.

- Your climb is
  rewarded by one of the best
  sections of downhill in the North
  West, as the route plunges
  1,000 feet into Alston. Near
  the bottom of Benty Hill there
  is a road on the right heading
  towards Leadgate and Garrigill.
  You have a choice – take it, or
  continue the delirious descent
  along the A686 until you get to
  the handsome town of Alston,
  perched on the edge of the
  Pennines.

ABOUT THE TOWN
Picture perfect legacy of the lead mines

Alston sits at 280m (919 feet) above sea level and is supposedly the highest market town in England. Picture-postcard-pretty and a firm favourite with outdoor types, it lies in an Area of Outstanding Natural Beauty (AONB), a solid bastion of civilisation on the edge of one of Britain's greatest areas of wilderness.

Once a centre for Cumberland wrestling, cattle fairs and races, Alston is unspoilt by developers and has cobbled streets, 17th century shops and pubs that hark back to a former age. Naturally it is a magnet for film makers; Oliver Twist was shot here for television – there is even an Oliver Twist trail – and Dickens himself visited in the 1830s to research Nicholas Nickleby.

The town, formed around the confluence of the South Tyne and Nent rivers, owes much to lead mining, started by the Romans before the Quakers set up the London Lead Mining Company in the 18th century. The Mines Heritage Centre has more information.

The mines and their machinery are silent but the scattered hill farms recall how mining families grew crops to subsidise their meagre wages.

The heather-clad moors, fells and valleys are alive with curlews, lapwings, peewits, peregrines and grouse, while deer and red squirrel roam this natural fastness.
There is some fine cycling across Alston Moor before you get to Nenthead. You can either take the B6277 past Garrigill or take the more direct A689.

🍴 WHERE TO EAT

Alston Wholefoods, Front Street
Run by: Local co-operative
Workers' co-operative, run by seven local people. Small local shop specialising in local products (especially cheese). Wide range of drinks, snacks, biscuits, local meats, gluten free items, soaps, candles, mustards, etc.
01434 381588
info@alstonwholefoods.com
alstonwholefoods.com

ALSTON HOUSE has been in the hands of seasoned chef, Michael Allchorne for nearly 10 years 01434 382200

BLUEBERRY'S in the Market Place – good meals, snacks and afternoon tea. See below for details 01434 381928.

THE CUMBERLAND HOTEL – see entry 01434 381875.

THE MOODY BAKER – artisan bakery owned by a workers' co-operative specialising in delicious pies, quiches etc and originators of the high-energy Moody Baker Biker Bar 01434 382003.

THE CUMBRIAN PANTRY, Front St. Good home baking. 01434 381406

 PLACES OF INTEREST

Tourist Information Centre: Town Hall, Front St. 01434 382244.

South Tynedale Railway Station: England's highest narrow-gauge track runs along 3.5 miles of former British Rail track bed. There is a tea room at the old station. Runs every weekend April - October plus some weekends in December, and daily during August. 01434 381696 or, for the talking timetable 01434 382828.

Hartside Nursery Garden: on route one mile from Alston. Rare and unusual alpine plants. 01434 381372.

The Hub, Station Unit, opposite rail station, Alston. Local history museum with eclectic mix. Entry by donation, run by volunteers. 01434 382244.

ACCOMMODATION

Alston Training & Adventure Centre, High Plains Lodge, CA9 3DD.
Run by: Dave Simpson
Ideal for campers or group bookings, though Alston Adventure Centre will accommodate individuals or small groups under the right circumstances. This is the ideal half-way stopping place, overlooking the Alston Valley with stunning views. Warm comfortable dormitories, lashings of food, a superb cooked breakfast, self-catering or camping option available.
Rooms: 10 sleeping 3 or more with total of 45 beds. 2 en-suite shower rooms.
Bed: £16 (bedding extra £6.25).
Breakfast: £6.50.
Eve meal: £11.
Pk lunch: £5.
Camping: £6.
Distance from route: 1.5 miles
B6277. 1 mile off-road.
Pub: 1 mile.
01434 381886
alstontraining@btconnect.com
alstontraining.co.uk

West Nattrass Tea Rooms & Guest House, Alston, CA9 3DA
Run by: Stephen & Gina Beimers

Former barn set in idyllic surroundings a mile up the Middleton road, taking the right fork at the top of the village. In the midst of open fells and wildflower meadows there are two en-suite guest rooms, secure lock-up and outbuildings for wet gear. The Beimers provide evening meals as well as a tea-room for hungry cyclists passing their door.

Rooms: 1T, 1D.
B&B: £35-£37.50 (£45 & £50 single occ).
Eve Meal: from £10.95. About £18 for 3-courses.
Pk lunch: £8.50.
01434 382292 / 07860 722151
info@westnattrass.com
westnattrass.com

Victoria Inn, Front St, Alston, CA9 3SE
Run by: Tian Smith

This is first and foremost a lively town centre pub (without music), with accommodation upstairs. It has been welcoming C2Cers for many years and Tian is a great host. But don't expect any frills and DO expect to find a real locals' bar - friendly and welcoming. The Victoria is warm, clean and comfortable offering everything you need. Accepts all major credit cards. Full Indian restaurant. Also doing takeaway. Sunday roasts. Really busy stop-off for C2Cers.

Rooms: 4S, 2D, 2F.
B&B: £30.
Packed lunch: from £3.50.
Eve meal: around £8. (Indian Restaurant)
01434 381194
victoriainncumbria@talk21.com

Alston House, Townfoot, Alston, CA9 3RN
Run by: Michael & Carole Allchorne

A restaurant with rooms very popular with cyclists - groups return year after year. 'We have lovely spotless rooms all with great views, modern bathrooms, some with roll top baths.' Great local ales and range of lagers, hearty homemade food and extensive menu cooked by Michael chef/owner whose generosity of portion is renowned. Sit in front of the fire or in the cafe with a latte, read the papers, or relax in the garden in the summer. 'We have lots of space and are ideal for groups. It's a lovely old building which has been lovingly updated.' The rest of Alston is just round the corner. There's a beauty room for massages and treatments.

Rooms: 5T, 2F.
B&B: £47.50-£50pppn.
Eve meal: 6-9pm £8-£18.
On route.
Fully licensed.
AA: 4-star 'Guest Accommodation'.
01434 382200
alstonhouse@fsmail.net
alstonhouse.co.uk

The Cumberland Inn, Townfoot, Alston, Cumbria CA9 3HX
Run by: Guy & Helen Harmer

Great for evening meals and simply wonderful for beer. Not for nothing was the Cumberland voted CAMRA Pub of the Year for the Solway region for the last several years on the trot. All rooms en-suite, bike storage, drying/cleaning facilities. Only stamping point in Alston. Choice of traditional cask ales and home cooked food. Family run and great cooking. Really friendly service and great atmosphere.

Rooms: 2D, 1F, 2Tpl.
B&B: £40. Single supplement £8.
Eve meal: £6-£15.
Pk lunch: £4.50.
VisitBritain: 3-star.
01434 381875
stay@cumberlandinnalston.co.uk
cumberlandinnalston.co.uk

YHA Alston, The Firs, Alston, Cumbria CA9 3RW
Run by: Linda Almond, Jenny Bradley & Neil Willmott

Alston Youth Hostel is a 30 bedded hostel providing 3-star affordable accommodation within 5 minutes walk of the town centre. All bed linen provided and all beds made up. Hot showers and excellent washing and drying facilities. Indoor secure cycle storage for 20 bikes. Superb selection of meals or self-catering option. Dining room to seats up to 30 people. Open all year round.

Rooms: 2x2, 2x4, 3x6 (bunkrooms).
Bed: from £20.50 (£16 for U-18).
Breakfast: £5.50 trad English.
Eve meal: £12 for 3 courses. £9.50 for 2.
Pk lunch: £5.

Secure cycle storage. On route.
Pubs serving food: 5-8 minute stroll..
01434 381509 / 07969655816
alston@yha.org.uk
alstonyouthhostel.co.uk

Lowbyer Manor Country House, Hexham Rd, Alston, CA9 3JX
Run by: Richard & Laura Elston

Grade II listed manor house in the heart of a UNESCO Area of Outstanding Natural Beauty. The C2C passes close by as well as several circular routes around the Alston area. AA Breakfast of the Year award. Cosy bar offering locally produced beers and soft drinks.

Rooms: 1S, 5D, 2T, 1F.
B&B: £39-£60.
Pk lunch: £5.
Distance from C2C: under 1km.
Same for pub.
AA 4 star 'Guest Accommodation'.
Secure cycle storage. Drying facilities.
Green Tourism Business
Scheme (GTBS), Gold Award.
01434 381230
stay@lowbyer.com
lowbyer.com

Town View, Camelot House, Alston, Cumbria CA9 3HS
Run by: Ted & Amanda

Luxurious private studio apartment ideal for a couple. Self-catering if you wish as Town View is self-contained and has been completely refurbished. Fully equipped kitchen, log burning stove and solid oak and leather furnishings right in the centre. Free Wifi and a 42" flat screen TV with 20 extra channels, films, Catch-Up TV etc. Everything is provided for your stay, all you need to do is turn up and relax. Free secure storage for bicycles and kit washing/drying service.

B&B: From £65 a night, room includes continental breakfast.
Rooms: studio apartment open plan.
Eve meal: self-catering or pubs
and restaurants in the vicinity.
Secure cycle storage
01434 382534 / 07903 923300
marketcrossalston@gmail.com
townviewalston.co.uk

···

Highfields, Bruntley Meadows, Alston, Cumbria CA9 3UX
Run by: Celia Pattison

Charming split level bungalow with sweeping views south west across the Cumbrian Fells. Celia has been looking after cyclists for 20 years now and provides a hearty supper and formidable breakfast (all the usual suspects and then some more). It's a leisurely stroll into town, past the police station and down to the Victoria or the Cumberland. Tea, coffee and home-made cakes on arrival.

Rooms: 1S, 1T, 1F.
B&B: £27.
Eve meal: £12 for 3 courses
Pk lunch: yes.
Secure space for bikes.
01434 382182
kalinkaleo@gmail.com

◎CYCLISTS◎
WELCOME WELCOME
◎CYCLISTS◎

GARRIGILL

The George & Dragon has reopened (again). There are plans to open rooms in time for next season and as we went to press the finishing touches were being put to a new kitchen, which will be turning out good local produce pub grub.

Garrigill is at the bottom of a perilously steep and winding lane as you head east along the C2C. Many cyclists have come to grief descending into the village and the helicopter ambulance is called out at least once a year to lift cyclists who have lost control, so be warned.

To get to Garrigill there is a clearly signed lane off to the right after Hartside, which also takes you to Leadgate. If you miss it, you will end up in Alston.

Garrigill once had a thriving population of 1,000 thanks to the lead mining. Now it is down to less than 200. It looks like the perfect English village, complete with green and post office. Some of the hardest riding is ahead, so for many it makes a natural overnight stop-off, especially if you have slogged all the way from the fells west of Penrith.

For those who like an extra challenge there is the tough route out of the village, up the very steep and rough track onto the B6277, then left onto a forest track and down into Nenthead the hard way.

ACCOMMODATION

Eastview, Garrigill, nr Alston, Cumbria CA93EA
Run by: Lana Dixie

Charming old cottage near the village green, recently and comfortably restored. Full English breakfast and fully geared up for cyclists. Plenty of books, games and maps and just a 30 second walk to the village pub, which is now under new management.

Rooms : 1D (en-suite), 1T.
B&B: £28 (£32 single occ and £35pp for the double).
Eve meal: George & Dragon.
Secure cycle lock-up. Drying facilities.
01434 381561
lanadixie@hotmail.com
garrigillbedandbreakfast.co.uk

....

George & Dragon, Garrigill, Alston, Cumbria CA9 3DS
Run by: Paula & Kenny

Lovely village pub on the green, now in the hands of Paula and Kenny, who took over in April 2015. They have plans to open bedrooms for next season. In the meantime the focus is on good pub food using local produce. There's a cheery hearth and care goes into serving some fine local ales. It is cheering to know that the heart of the village is beating once more. Food available from June.

Lunches and dinners served.

Secure bike shed with repair area.
01434 381900
thegeorgeanddragoninn@gmail.com
garrigillpub.co.uk

NENTHEAD

ABOUT THE VILLAGE

Folk in both Nenthead and Allenheads - the next port of call - claim to live in England's highest village. I would be interested to know definitively which is the higher. Either way, Nenthead is 500m above sea level and has a colder climate than Aberdeen. It does seem incredible that only 300 million years ago it was on the equator.

The village was purpose-built for mining in 1825 by the Quaker Lead Company. In addition to housing they provided a reading room, wash-house, public baths and a school for the 1500 employees in the Methodist stronghold. At weekends they ran smallholdings and this way of life lasted for more than 100 years. A decorative fountain in the middle of the village serves as a memorial to R.W.Bainbridge Esq, superintendent of the mine company.

Falling markets destroyed the community, with cheap imports leading to a collapse in prices, and many families emigrated to the USA and Australia at the end of the 19th century. Zinc mining continued until the 1940s and Nenthead Mines eventually closed its last pit in 1961.

 ## ACCOMMODATION

The Miners Arms, Nenthead, CA9 3PF

Run by: Alison Clark

Recently voted the 'Greenest Pub In Britain' after winning its Green Tourism Gold Star. Excellent food and good beer at the pub which lays claim to being the highest in England. The new luxury en-suite accommodation was amongst the 2012 Top 10 B&Bs in Cumbria in The Times travel section. Alison has run the Miners since 1988, adding a conservatory dining room. Member of the Green Tourism scheme promoted by the AONB

Rooms: 2T, 1T/Tpl.
B&B: from £25.
Eve meal: £7.50-£15.
Pk lunch: £4.

Secure storage.
Green Tourism Gold Award.
Drying facilities.
VisitBritain: 3-star.
01434 381427 / 07817 615417
theminersarms2@gmail.com
nenthead.com

Lovelady Shield

Run by: Marie & Peter Haynes

In this rugged section of the ride lies an oasis of comfort and calm: Lovelady Shield, an elegant Georgian former shooting lodge on the banks of the river Nent. Award winning food and three acres of secluded gardens in which to sit and relax after the ups and downs. Ideal for groups as there are three cottages as well as 12 bedrooms. Cocktail bar, library and lounge with log fires. The highlight for many is dinner, served in an elegant dining room. The menu varies daily and is imaginatively prepared by the longstanding master chef, Barrie Garton.

Rooms: 4T/D, 8D.
Three cottages: sleep 4/6 & 8.
B&B: from £35.
Dinner: from £27.50.
Pk lunch: by prior arrangement.
Fully licensed.
01434 381203
enquiries@lovelady.co.uk
lovelady.co.uk

Haggs Bank Bunkhouse, Nentsberry, Alston, Cumbria CA9 3LH

Run by: Cathy Reynolds & Danny Taylor

Great addition to the route - terraced campsite and bunkhouse ideal for self-catering groups of up to 24, though meals can be pre-ordered (from £6 - look out for Cathy's cakes). Charming spot and beautifully converted bunkhouse with ample washrooms. Towel hire possible. Three bunkrooms sleeping 10, 9 and 5. Largest one has en-suite facilities. BBQ for hire and also a firepit.

Bunkrooms sleep 10,9 & 5.
Bed: £18.
Whole bunkhouse: £380 per night.
Campsite has 12 hook-ups for motorhomes.
Secure lock-up.
01434 382486 / 07919 092403
info@haggsbank.com
haggsbank.com/bunkhouse

Nent Hall Country House Hotel & Farmhouse B&B, Nent Hall, CA9 3LQ

Run by: Adele Phillips & Pamela Kent

A bit of luxury at the end of a hard day in the saddle? Here you have it, with a pub attached, the Coach House. In addition to a good pint, main courses go from £8, not to mention afternoon tea for those wanting to pop in for sustenance before the climbs ahead. Look out for great online deals at the hotel. Cycle friendly and stylish, attractive setting in affordable country house accommodation. A splendid setting just off the A689, about 1.5 miles west of Nenthead.

Rooms: 4S/D, 2T, 2F, 6 four-posters, 2 superior 4-poster, five room suite.
B&B hotel: from £30.
D,B&B: from £47.
Eve meals: bar meals from £8 - £15.
Restaurant: 3 courses from £25.
Pk lunch: by arrangement.
01434 381584
info@nenthall.com
nenthall.com

Mill Cottage, Nenthead, Cumbria CA9 3PD

Run by: Phil & Julie Jones

Quality bunkhouse accommodation by Nenthead Mines on the route. Sole use of the bunkhouse cannot be guaranteed for your group unless you arrange this with us in advance. Each bed is styled like a ship's cabin bunk with blinds for privacy and a small internal light and shelf. Downstairs is a sitting room / dining room. The bunkhouse is fully heated, has hot water and two showers. The Miners Arms does evening meals (01434 381427). Please book in advance, especially for groups.

Rooms: 1 bunkhouse sleeps 6. Bed (and self-catering b'fast): £18.

Eve meal: Miners Arms pub.

Pk lunch: by arrangement.

Kitchen: cooker, fridge/freezer, microwave, toaster etc.

Utility/washing room with washing machine & tumble dryer.

Bedding is provided (duvet, pillow & sheets).

Towels on request.

Secure cycle storage.

01434 381674

millcottagenenthead@gmail.com

millcottagebunkhouse.co.uk

⊚ CYCLE REPAIRS

North Pennine Cycles, run by Dave Raeside, will repair, fine-tune or even replace your bike, should the rigours of the journey require. This excellent resource is now firmly established as one of the best in the north.

• Fully Park Tool equipped, with a wide range of parts and accessories. (All major brands)

• Cycle nutrition and energy drinks.

• Rescue and call-out service with 3-bike rack.

• Cycle hire including: Tandem and Electric Bikes!

• Reasonable rates and fast action.

• Cytech 2 qualified mechanic.

01434 381324 | northpenninecycles@gmail.com

www.northpenninecycles.co.uk | Nenthead, Cumbria CA9 3PF

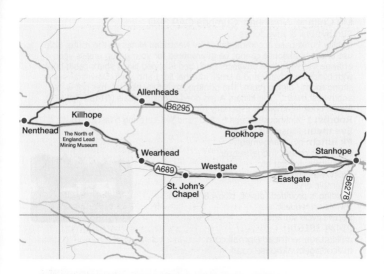

WEARDALE ALTERNATIVE

Nenthead > Killhope North of England Lead Mining Museum: 3 miles

Killhope > Cowshill: 2.8 miles (5.8)

Cowshill > St John's Chapel: 2.8 miles (8.6)

St John's Chapel > Westgate: 1.6 miles (10.2)

Westgate > Eastgate: 3.3 miles (13.5)

Eastgate > Stanhope: 3.2 miles (16.7)

The Weardale Alternative takes you over the highest A road in England, through a series of picturesque villages at the head of the River Wear and along the prettiest seven mile back road, returning you to the official route in the market town of Stanhope.

It offers a much-needed alternative to the main route, where it is sometimes difficult to find accommodation and food. 'We simply cannot cope with the demand', is an oft-heard refrain, though the Herculean efforts made by the Allenheads Inn come in for high praise.

Unlike the splendid isolation of the official route via Allenheads and Rookhope, Upper Weardale offers you cafés, convenience stores, museums and a range of accommodation, from camping to a luxury country house hotel.

From Nenthead, simply carry on the main road over the three-hump hill of Killhope Cross (647m) and enjoy the exhilarating downhill stretch into Weardale. If you find the hills of the North Pennines hard, you may want to stop off at Killhope Lead Mining Museum to experience something of how life was for those working in and under the hills – and get a coffee while there, from the Café.

The villages of Lanehead, Cowshill and Wearhead line the route to Ireshopeburn, home of The Weardale Museum, which is brim full of fascinating insights into how life was when Weardale was a hive of mining and Methodism.

Chatterbox Café in St John's Chapel hosts the Upper Weardale Visitor Information Point and Weardale Bike Hire. As well as being a perfect place to rest up before Crawleyside Bank, it also provides info on the eating and sleeping places in the dale and route maps for cycling challenges you may want to attempt on a return visit – including over Chapelfell, the highest road in the country.

Half a mile down the valley in Daddry Shield, The Weardale Alternative turns off the main road and down a beautiful back road wending its way alongside the river, past the Hare and Hounds pub in Westgate, and the 5 star luxury hotel of Horsely Hall before recrossing the river in Stanhope and you're back on the official route.

🍴 WHERE TO EAT

The North of England Lead Mining Museum, Near Cowshill, Upper Weardale, Co Durham DL13 1AR

Run by: Pip Gill

Great pit-stop on the new Weardale Alternative, Pip and her team welcome you to Killhope Café. Offering a wonderful menu from 10.30 (last orders: 4pm) with a choice of home-made soups, sandwiches, scones, cakes and lots more. Come in for lunch or just a relaxing cuppa. Ingredients are organic and/or locally sourced where possible. Caters for groups. Ask Pip about her special group deals. Al fresco dining! With funding from Leader, the cafe now has an awning over its picnic area. **Killhope Museum** is open daily 11-5 until Nov. Admission tickets valid for a year. Underground tours and a wealth of wildlife including red squirrels can be observed on the woodland trails. Award winning staff will answer all your questions about life at the top of the dale in the 19th C and ensure a memorable visit.

Serving from 10.30am until 5.00pm daily (until Nov).

Last order for meals: 4pm.

Visitor information. Bike storage.
Ideal for groups and a good place
for back-up teams to hang out.
01388 537 505
info@killhope.org.uk
killhope.org.uk

Chatterbox Cafe, 11 Market Pl, St John's Chapel, Bishop Auckland DL13 1QF

Run by: Cameron and Anne Marie Gordon

Splendid new addition to the Weardale stretch of the ride, offering emergency relay, spares and bike hire. The owner, Cameron, is a keen cyclist and veteran of the C2C. Hot and cold food - anything from cheesy beans on toast to all-day-breakfasts to locally made soups. And there's always homemade flapjack, chocolate bars and peanut butter and jam sandwiches for calorie cravers.

Open Every Day from at least 9am-5pm.
Free coffee and tea refills.
Dry Bike Storage. Bike hire. Emergency relay.
Spares service. Cycle route maps and advice.
Visitor Information.
01388 537536
cafe@stjohnschapel.co.uk
stjohnschapel.co.uk

....

The Blue Bell Inn, 12 Hood St, St Johns Chapel, DL13 1QJ.

Run by: Bryan & Kath

Once a pair of terraced stone cottages, the pub has undergone a transformation into a chapel of worship for beer drinkers. One of only two Cask Marque outlets in the area, Bryan and Kath go to great pains to ensure their regularly changing ales are in top condition. Most are from mocrobreweries nearby. Kath pickles the eggs.

Pool room and beer garden.
Weekdays 5-12.
Weekends 12-12.
Will open up if you're thirsty
01388 537256
bluebellin@outlook.com

....

Pennine Lodge, St. Johns Chapel, Bishop Auckland, DL13 1QX

Run by: Joyce Walton

Luxury 1-room B&B plus campsite on the banks of the Wear in 16 acres of private land, this is a relaxing, tranquil environment in the heart of Weardale AONB, where, if you have the energy you can walk, fish on their stretch of the river or visit the alpaca herd. The B&B is newly renovated to a luxury standard, complete with TV, tea/coffee making facilities, en-suite, private entrance, patio and seating area. Part of Camping and Caravanning Club, 10 pitches and 5 caravans.

B&B: £75 (£55 single occ). £65 room only.
Room: 1 D.
Tents: £6.
Caravans: £8.
Eve meal: Golden Lion or Blue Bell.
Pk lunch: pse pre-order.
Secure cycle storage.
01388 537946
penninelodgeweardale@gmail.com
penninelodgeweardale.co.uk

ACCOMMODATION

Dales Farm, High Copthill, Cowshill DL13 1AD
Run by: Anita & Terry Holmes
Old farmhouse originally dating from the 16th century, with all the modern comforts and in 10 acres of farmland. Anita provides evening meals often including home-reared Black Wensleydale lamb. Hearty portions and there's an off-licence and pub just down the road.
Rooms: 2D.
B&B: £65-£75 per room.
Single occ: £55-£65.
Eve meal: £15 for 2-courses, £18 for 3.
Pk lunch: yes.
Secure cycle storage
(lockable shed inside a lockable barn!)
Drying facilities.
01388 537987 / 07785 282293
info@dalesfarm.net
dalesfarm.net

....

The Golden Lion, 12 Market Place, St John's Chapel DL13 1 QF
Run by: Glen & Caroline Royston
18th century coaching inn bang on the new route offering a bespoke service for C2Cers. At time of going to press bunkhouses were being prepared (to sleep 10) plus five guest rooms. The Roystons, who serve good real ale, are keen to promote cycling in the new hub of activity that is St John's Chapel. Good food at reasonable prices.
Rooms: 4/5 S/D/T.
Bunkrooms: 2 sleeping total of 10 £20.
B&B: from £30.
Eve meals: from £8 (local produce).
Pk lunch: pse preorder.
Secure lock-up and drying facilities.
01388 537231 / 07736 672677
goldenlionstjohnschapel@btconnect.com
thegoldenlionweardale.com

....

Bridge House, 2 Hood St, St Johns Chapel, DL13 1QB
Run by: Roger & Fiona Chambers
Comfortable end of terrace house with great views over Harthope Burn, one of the Wear's main tributaries. Lovingly renovated with two king-size rooms with twin split options, there is free wifi and satellite TV plus the Golden Lion and Chatterbox cafe nearby.
Rooms: 2 T/D (zip lock kingsize beds).
B&B: £26 to £31.50.
Single occ: £40 or £50.
Eve meal: Golden Lion or Chatterbox.
Pk lunch: £5.
Secure lock-up and drying facilities.
01388 537983 / 07906 687109
bridgehousestjohnschapel@btinternet.com
harle-southern.com

Westgate Manor, Westgate, Weardale DL13 1JT
Run by: Kathryn & Stuart Dobson

Beautifully and sympathetically restored Victorian manor house set in the middle of the AONB. It's a five minute stroll to the pub if you can wrench yourself away from the lovely grounds and comfort of the house. Afternoon teas, lunches and dinners served. Log burners and antiques, hot baths and great service.

Rooms: 4/5. There is a family suite comprising 1D and 1T with a shared bathroom. 4D, including a 4-poster!

B&B: from £44.50pppn.
Family suite: £179.
4-poster: £104 and £119.
Eve meal: yes - please pre-book or use nearby pub.
Pk lunch: please pre-order.
Secure cycle storage. Drying facilities.
01388 537231 / 07736 672677
info@westgatemanor.co.uk
westgatemanor.co.uk

....

Hill House East Country B&B, Westgate, DL13 1NU
Run by: Carol & John Graham

Renowned for its hospitality and fine, hearty fare, the Grahams run a top class B&B and are tailor-made for C2Cers. 'We don't do portion control,' says Carol. Country supper includes lamb broth, home baked bread and scones, and there are home-grown eggs for breakfast. Expect to revisit as many of their bookings are from repeat visitors. Afternoon tea is included on arrival.

Rooms: 1D, 1T.
B&B (plus afternoon tea): from £35.
Eve meal: £15.
Pk lunch: £5.
Secure lock-up and drying facilities.
01388 517145
enquiries@hillhouseeast.co.uk
hillhouseeast.co.uk

ALLENHEADS

This is an unremitting stretch with the steepest climb directly out of Nenthead, so if you are staying overnight you may wish to sidestep one of those typically generous Cumbrian breakfasts.

Turn left off the A689 after just over a kilometre of steep gradient, past the disused lead mineshafts, and soon you will be crossing the highest point on the route – Black Hill. At 609 metres (just a tad under 2000 feet) it is 29 metres (nearly 100 feet) higher than Hartside. Once you have conquered the climb past Killhope Law it's plain sailing to Allenheads.

This is a delightful village nestling among the trees. Its focal point is a marvellous little pub called the Allenheads Inn, one of the most popular stop-off points anywhere along the route.

A century ago this prosperous, peaceful little haven was a toneless grey valley of slag heaps shrouded by smog, a mining community that provided one sixth of the nation's lead. It slipped into decline along with the industry, but has revitalised itself. There is now a village Trust, a visitor centre, mining exhibitions, a shop and a café. It is also home to the British Norwegian Ski Club. There are three tow ropes on the run to the top at 540 metres. Annual family membership is £30.

 ## PLACES OF INTEREST

Woodland Nature Trail - walks that take you around the village.

Old Blacksmith's Shop - smithy with display.

The Allenheads Trust, Allenheads Heritage Centre 01434 685043

 ## ACCOMMODATION

The Allenheads Inn, Allenheads, nr Hexham, NE47 9HJ
Run by: Ann & Phil Homer
Right on the original C2C route, this is a lovely 18th century village inn and a must for cyclists who enjoy atmosphere, hospitality and all-round rustic comfort. Fine ales and huge helpings of tasty fare make this probably the most popular stop-off on the entire route. CAMRA and Good Pub Guide. Single occupancy restricted during busy season. Dinners from £7.99 up to £15.99 for a 12oz plate defying sirloin. Secure lock-up, free parking, free wifi.
Rooms: 2D, 5T, 1F.
B&B: £39. Single occ. £49.
Eve meal: yes.
Pk lunch: £5.50.
Open all year.
Secure cycle parking.
01434 685200
philann@phomer.fsbusiness.co.uk
allenheadsinn.co.uk

Thorn Green Accommodation, Thorn Green, Allenheads, NE47 9JQ

Run by: Julie Macdonald

Bunkhouse and campsite right on C2C route about 1.5 miles before Allenheads Village. There are 2 rooms in the Bunkhouse, each sleeping 6 people. The campsite is small but secluded right at the back of the Bunkhouse. There are showers and a locked bike shed for the Bunkhouse. No kitchen facilities and booking is essential. Evening meals available in the village.

Rooms: 2 - 6 bunks each + 2 showers.
Camping: £7 pppn.
B&B: £27.

Packed lunch: Please give a day
or so advance warning.
On C2C route.
Pub: in the village.
Drying facilities and secure lock-up.
01434 685234 \ 07977 728328
thorngreen@live.co.uk
thorngreenaccommodation.co.uk

Allenheads Lodge, Allenheads, NE47 9HW

Run by: Sarah Marriner
Central heating, secure bike lockup, drying room, separate showers. 4 bed new self-catering cottage to rent next to Allenheads Lodge.
Rooms: 4 (total of 24 beds).
Bed only: £19.50
B&B: £25.
Pk lunch: £4.50.
Eve meal: on request.
On C2C route.
Pub: 700m.
0191 564 0291
smarriner@springboard-ne.org
springboard-ne.org

Newhouses, Allenheads, Northumberland NE47 9HX

Run by: Pat & Terry McMullon

Newhouses was built in 1788 by Sir Thomas Blackett. Standing 1400 feet above sea level, it was originally a short row of cottages provided for workers in the Allenheads Leadmines. Warm and comfortable with fantastic views over the fells and open all year, there are 5 beds in 2 twins and a single room. One is en-suite while the other shares a bathroom with the single room. We live in the adjoining cottage but you have your own sitting room, dining room and kitchen.

Rooms: 1S/D, 2T.
B&B: £30-£35.
Pk lunch: from £4.
On C2C route.
Drying facilities.
Secure lock-up.
01434 685260
zookon@aol.com
allenheadsc2c.com

The Old School House , Allenheads, NE47 9HR
Run by: Helen Ratcliffe & Alan Smith
The Victorian Schoolhouse has a newly refurbished accommodation wing
which includes a large open plan area with big comfy sofas, wood burning
stove and built in kitchen.   Approx 100 metres from C2C route and pub
with spectacular views over village and North Pennines.
B&B: £30 - £35.
Rooms: 2T and 2 bunk rooms (4 beds in each).
Max 12 beds. 2 bathrooms with shower.
Pk lunch: no.
Eve meal: pub.
Secure cycle storage.
01434 685040 \ 07966 257276
helenshead@acart.org.uk
acart.org.uk/allenheadsaccommodation.html

WHERE TO EAT

Hemmel Cafe, Allenheads
Run by: Amanda Noble
The Hemmel Cafe is a charming little stop-off with a wood-burning stove, an
airy courtyard and free WiFi. Amanda Noble, who took over in 2013, offers
home cooking using seasonal, locally sourced ingredients and teas, coffees,
wines and bottled beers. Breakfast is served all day and the home-made
bread, scones and cakes are to die for.
Amanda has injected much energy to this
thriving hub.
Main courses: £6.25 to £7.95.
April 1 to Sept 30 open every day 9-5;
Oct 1 to Mar 31 open 10-4 (except Wed).
01434 685568
amanda@thehemmelcafe.co.uk
thehemmelcafe.co.uk

ALLENHEADS ➜ STANLEY OR ROWLANDS GILL

Allenheads to Stanley: 32 miles (16 miles traffic-free)

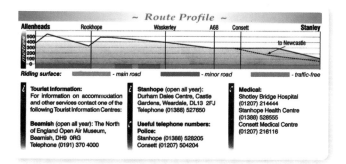

~ *Route Profile* ~

Riding surface: ▬▬▬ - main road ▬▬▬ - minor road ▬▬▬ - traffic-free

i **Tourist Information:**
For information on accommodation and other services contact one of the following Tourist Information Centres:

Beamish (open all year): The North of England Open Air Museum, Beamish, DH9 0RG
Telephone (0191) 370 4000

i **Stanhope** (open all year):
Durham Dales Centre, Castle Gardens, Weardale, DL13 2FJ
Telephone (01388) 527650

Useful telephone numbers:
Police:
Stanhope (01388) 528205
Consett (01207) 504204

Medical:
Shotley Bridge Hospital
(01207) 214444
Stanhope Health Centre
(01388) 528555
Consett Medical Centre
(01207) 216116

ROOKHOPE

The stretch out of Allenheads is second from last serious ascent - and it drags on until you reach the summit at Currick. Then there is a nice stretch of gentle downhill all the way to Rookhope. You soon pass the boundary into County Durham, land of the Prince Bishops, local rulers who exercised absolute authority, equal to a sovereign within the principality. They were granted such power because of the huge strategic importance of the area in the ongoing battle with the Scots.

On your approach you will pass the Lintzgarth Arch, an incongruous and enormous vestige of a bygone era, lying abandoned on the valley floor. The arch carried a 3km horizontal chimney across the valley which replaced the more conventional vertical type when it was realised that a lot of lead literally went up with the smoke. Consequently teams of chimneysweeps were employed to scrape the valuable lead and silver deposits from the chimney once a week. It was a dangerous and filthy job, done by children.

Rookhope is another shrunken mining village. It is also charming, keeping the secret of its hiding place well guarded from sight high above the Weardale Valley. It is hard to imagine that this small group of dwellings was a hive of activity only a few years ago.

In its heyday it supported a surgery, a resident district nurse, vicar, policeman, teashops, several crowded pubs and a busy school. The mining of lead, iron and fluorspar, smelting and the railways totally dominated people's lives.

Today the village is a welcome watering hole and resting place for weary cyclists before the final leg of the C2C journey down to the NE coast. Now there is only a pub (pleasantly refurbished), village shop, post office and working man's club - but a splendid stopping off point, nonetheless.

 # ACCOMMODATION

Barrington Bunkhouse, Rookhope-in-Weardale, Co. Durham, DL13 2BG

Run by: Valerie Livingston

Barrington Bunkhouse is both homely and cosy, offering a warm welcome to C2Cers. It is directly on the route and right next door to The Rookhope Inn, which offers good beer and substantial fare. The communal bunkroom consists of 6 bunks, one fold-out bed, and a seating area in the middle of the room. There is a self-serve continental breakfast from a well stocked kitchen. There are 2 showers, 2 toilets, one with disabled facilities, a tumble dryer, secure bike storage, and an attractive patio. The owners are a musical bunch, so musicians are very welcome to borrow a guitar and have a go!

B&B: £22.

Camping: £14 with breakfast (£10 without).

Drying: tumble dryer plus oil-filled radiators.
Secure lock-up for bikes.

01388 517656
barrington_bunkhouse@hotmail.co.uk
barrington-bunkhouse-rookhope.com

....

2 Princess Cottages, Rookhope, DL13 2BP

Run by: Mary Auckland

Charming old 2-bedroom cottage within stumbling distance of the pub. The owners live across the road so there's privacy. It comprises two twin rooms, shower room and a living room with coal fire, plus kitchenette (so you could buy food in Alston and cook it here). Dinner is provided on request. Secure lock up for bikes. Continental breakfast provided.

Rooms: 2T

B&B: £30

Eve meal: yes but you must order.
£10 for 2 courses..

Pk lunch: yes on request.
Secure lock-up.
01388 517930
mary@stayinrookhope.co.uk

Rookhope Bunkhouse, Fellhouse, Rookhope, Co Durham DL13 2BD
Run by: Iain & Shayne Smith
Charming 19th century cottage on the fell overlooking the village, just a
few minutes walk from the pub, which serves good food and good beer.
Sleeps eight in two bunk rooms. This new bunkhouse is on the track
leading to the grouse moor and the off-road section and offers comfort
and value for money. Continental breakfast. There is a small kitchen area
downstairs, along with a shower and wc. There is also onsite camping and
special offers for those staying for several nights.
B&B: £22.
Rooms: 1X6; 1X2.
Eve meal: pub.
Pk lunch: £5.
Drying facilities. Secure lock-up.
01388 517927 / 07909 443866
bookings@fellhousecottage.co.uk
fellhousecottage.co.uk

EASTGATE

To get to Eastgate for those heading towards Hole House
Bunkhouse and the comforts of the Cross Keys, take Route 7
signs for Stanhope. Just outside Rookhope you will see that the
C2C branches off to the left: ignore, and continue straight on,
soon crossing the Rookhope Burn. It's a couple of miles down to
the village and then a couple of miles east to Stanhope, where
you rejoin the official route. As accommodation in this wonderfully
remote part of the world is limited, the addition of Hole House is
indeed welcome.

ACCOMMODATION

Cross Keys, Eastgate, Weardale, Co Durham DL13 2HW

Run by: Gaynor and Brian Irwin

Friendly country inn with lots of character the cross keys dates back to 1617 and is a real gem of a traditional co Durham pub. The rooms have recently been refurbished to a comfortable and high standard and all have en-suite, central heating, flat screen TV, tea & coffee making facilities. Enjoy a drink in the bar by the open fire, or have a meal in the dining room. The Cross Keys enjoys catering for cyclists. Dogs welcome, but not allowed in the bedrooms.

Rooms: 4T/D (zip-link into K-size doubles).
2F with 4S. Up to 16 adults catered for
in single beds.
B&B: £32.50 to £60 (single occ.)
Family rooms £110
Lunch and eve meals:
yes - from £6 to £13.50.
Pk lunch: by arrangement.
Secure lock up. Drying facilities.
01388 517234 \ 07881 553454
info@crosskeyseastgate.co.uk
crosskeyseastgate.co.uk

....

Hole House Bunkhouse B&B, Weardale DL13 2HX

Run by: Lizzie & Sophie Jackson

Bunkhouse located on a small farm just 5 minutes walk to the local Crosskeys Inn. Evening meal can be provided if required if you do not fancy the trip down to the pub. Good clean accommodation with attached large kitchen and TV room. Great quiet location with secure bike storage/workshop.

Rooms: 3 quad rooms, ie 2 pairs of bunks in each room - all en-suite.

B&B: £20 per person.
Eve meal: £10 (please pre-order food
and refreshments).
Pk lunch: £4.50 (please pre-book).
Secure cycle parking.
0.5 miles from alternative route.
Pub: 0.5 miles.
01388 517311 / 07968 204599
holehousebunks@btinternet.com

STANHOPE

- From Rookhope you can take the exciting but demanding off-road section which climbs steeply past ruins and heads along the edge of Edmundbyers Common, leading down to the Waskerley Way either by road or across a track – the choice is yours.

- The second choice is to go via Stanhope, one of Weardale's more important and historic little market towns. But if you go this way, remember that you'll be facing a swine of a climb up the B6278 to the Waskerley Way, aptly called Crawley Side.

ABOUT THE AREA

Sleepy backwater that reaped the rail reward

Originally a Bronze Age settlement, it was a tiny village around a cobbled market square until the Stanhope & Tyne Railway was built to transport the industrial produce to Consett and Cleveland along the Waskerley Way.

Before the railways, all raw materials were transported by pack horses. Teams of tough little Galloway horses would pick their way over the Pennines and then down into the valleys, the lead horse often having a bell attached to its harness to guide the following horses across the mist-cloaked moors.

PLACES OF INTEREST

Durham Dales Visitor Centre

Castle Gardens. Delightful café.
01388 527 650.

Fossilised tree at St Thomas's Church 350 million years old, found in 1914 in an Edmundbyers mine.

St Thomas's Church 12th century origins complete with Roman altar and Saxon font.

ACCOMMODATION

Red Lodge, 2 Market Place, Stanhope DL13 2UN
Run by: Dawn & Andy Clarke
Under new ownership from 2014, this is a warm and welcoming B&B, an ideal place to relax in before the final day of the C2C. Red Lodge is a 200 year old former hunting lodge in the heart of Weardale's charming market town of Stanhope and is noted for its excellent breakfasts, comfort and superbly appointed en-suite bedrooms. It is also perfectly located within a stone's throw of all of the local amenities including four excellent, friendly pubs. Free wifi. Washing and drying facilities available.
Rooms: 1T, 1D/S, 1King.
B&B: from £40pp. Single occ. £50.
Eve meal: no - plenty of pubs nearby.
Pk lunch: yes. Secure cycle storage.
01388 526152 / 07429 521914
RedLodge_Stanhope@Outlook.com
redlodgebnb.com

The Packhorse Inn, 8 Market Place, Stanhope
Co Curham, DL13 2ES

Run by: Sarah Roper & Colin Emerson

Rapidly gaining popularity amongst the cycling fraternity, making it an ideal C2C stopover. Sarah and Colin are keen to keep it cycle-friendly, offering traditional bar meals, with real ales. Comfortable and competitively priced rooms with secure storage for your cycles overnight. Large group room & twin rooms for cycle parties of up to 14 people with Friday and Saturday night entertainment. Give yourself a real head-start with a hearty full English breakfast. A Warm and Friendly welcome awaits you.

Rooms: 1F (sleeps 8), 1D/T, 2T
B&B: £30, Single £45.
(£50 Bank Holidays)
Eve meal: Pre-book.
Pk lunch: Pre-book.
Secure lock up.
Washing & drying facilities upon request.
01388 528407
c2c@packhorsestanhope.co.uk
packhorsestanhope.co.uk

....

Grey Bull, 17 West Terrace, Stanhope, Co Durham DL13 2PB

Run by: Diane Garbutt & Stuart Brown

Diane and Stuart who used to be at the Bonny Moorhen have now taken over this lovely old pub with open fires and real ales. It's been refurbished with a 10-bed bunkhouse and is ideally placed at the foot of Crawleyside. Continental breakfast and free takeaway delivery service for pizzas, Indian and Chinese meals. Ideally located at the foot of Crawleyside Bank for the last big haul of the ride.

Rooms: 1 X 10-bed bunkhouse.
B&B: £25.
Secure cycle storage.
01388 529428 / 07885 676575
diane.garbutt@hotmail.com

....

The Bonny Moor Hen, 25 Front St, Stanhope, Co Durham

Run by: Trevor Hudspeth & Gwen Varley

Can take groups of up to 15 if you don't mind sharing the occasional double bed. Bustling pub in the centre of Stanhope, rapidly gaining in popularity among the cycling fraternity. Secure lock up and reasonably priced home cooked food. Now under new management, there is a full menu offering pies, steaks, fish, curries and much more. Meal deal: 2 for £10. Live entertainment every weekend. Music finishes at 11.45pm on Saturday.

Rooms: 1 (1D+3S), 2F (1D+1S), 2T.
Most en-suite.
B&B: £35.
Eve meal: Yes - BOOKING
ESSENTIAL Sat & Sun.
Pk lunch: yes.
On route. Secure storage.
Washing & drying facilities.
01388 528214
thebonnymoorhen@outlook.com
bonnymoorhen.co.uk

Parkhead Station, Stanhope Moor, Co. Durham DL13 2ES

Run by: Terry & Lorraine Turnbull

On the moor 3 miles out of Stanhope, at the top of Crawleyside and 10 miles before Consett, Parkhead is a haven built for cyclists. Bang on the 100-mile marker (it's all downhill from here!) Parkhead is well known within the cycling fraternity for its good home-cooked food, licensed bar, tranquil location and service tailor-made for the cyclist's needs. The Tea Rooms are often bustling with folk taking a well earned break in our Tea Rooms. The B&B rooms are comfortable and all command great views over the North Pennines. Evening meal available for non-residents. Lorraine, who runs it with husband Terry, used to work for Sustrans and was involved with the C2C since the start.

Rooms: 2D, 3F. Tea & coffee facilities, flat screeen TV/DVD.

B&B: from £30.

Eve meal: pre-ordering essential. Locally sourced produce. Contact us for menu choices and dietary requirements.
Pk lunch: £3.50.
Licensed. On route.
VisitBritain: 3 stars.
01388 526434
parkheadstation@aol.com
parkheadstation.co.uk

· ·

Horsley Hall, Eastgate, Bishop Auckland, Co Durham, DL13 2LJ

Run by: Mrs Liz Curry

Good for groups up to 16, and built originally in the 14th century as the Prince Bishop of Durham's hunting lodge, a warm welcome awaits you at ivy-clad Horsley Hall Country House. Now a family run hotel and set in picturesque Weardale only a mile or so from the route, it is on a back road loop from Rookhope to Stanhope and is a great place to celebrate your last night in style. Relax by the log fires in the lounge and dine in splendour in the Baronial Hall, which can seat up to 50. All food is home cooked and locally sourced, professionally produced by Liz who is a trained master chef. Luxury accommodation caters for 12 guests. All bedrooms are en-suite with both showers & baths. Licensed bar.

Rooms: 4T, 1S, 2D.
B&B: from £57.50 if sharing.
Eve meal: from £14. 3 courses from £20, pre-booking recommended.
Lunch: from £10.50.
Pk lunch: from £4.50.

Secure lock up. Wash down facilities.
VisitBritain 5-stars Silver Award.
Taste of Durham.
Licensed bar and wine cellar.
01388 517239
info@horsleyhall.co.ukco.uk
horsleyhall.co.uk

WIGGO'S WAY

This new alternative route has just been added. It avoids the bottleneck at Rookhope and the haul across to Allenheads. There is much to be said for it, on the grounds of breathtaking scenery, new challenges and also for the wonderful communities along the route. There are lots of places to stop off, whether it be the postcard-pretty village of Askham or the handsome medieval town of Appleby. This new braid, named by locals in honour of Sir Bradley Wiggins, will prove a popular alternative.

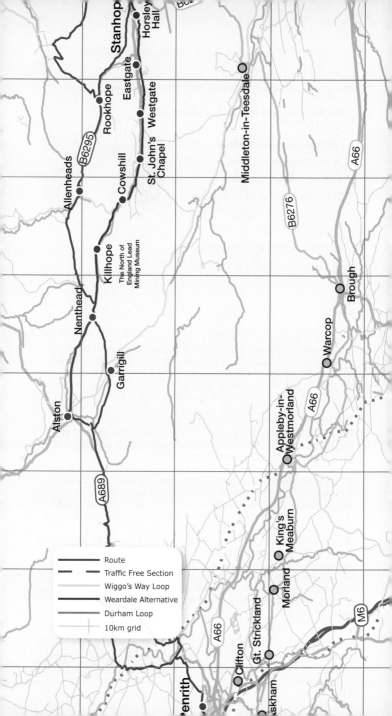

PENRUDDOCK → STANHOPE

Via Appleby and Middleton: 58 miles.

Penruddock > Pooley Bridge: 5.2 miles

Pooley Bridge > Askham: 3.7 miles (8.9)

Askham > Great Strickland: 3.7 miles (12.6)

Great Strickland > King's Meaburn: 4.7 miles (17.3)

King's Meaburn > Appleby: 5.3 miles (22.6)

Appleby > Brough: 8.3 miles (30.9)

Brough > Middleton-in-Teesdale: 14.2 (45.1)

Middleton-in-Teesdale > Stanhope: 12.8 (57.9)

▶ ROUTE DESCRIPTION

- From Troutbeck follow C2C route for 1.5 miles to the point where you turn left at the pub. Here you carry straight on to Penruddock. Ignoring the left turn to Motherby, go to the T-junction and head left to the A66, turning briefly right then, 1st left to Hutton, passing through the village, before turning right at Hutton John.

- Continue along the lane, ignoring the right fork to Thackthwaite. Passing the village of Wreay you will turn left onto the A592 up to the B5320, going through Pooley Bridge and continue for less than a mile before taking a right to Celleron and Askham.

- In Askham, head left keeping the Punchbowl on your right, heading towards Lowther. Cross the river Lowther and keep left and you will see the castle. Either head to the hamlet of Lowther or keep left and you will very briefly find yourself on the A6, which you need to cross.

- Go under the railway line. Shortly after is a right turn to Gt Strickland, where there is excellent overnight accommodation at the Strickland Arms. If you wish to carry on and link up again with the C2C at Penrith, follow Pennine Cycleway signs (Route 67). From the Cross Keys either go into the town centre and pick up signs, or very briefly go right on the A686 before taking a left up to Beacon Hill and back onto the route.

ASKHAM

Askham is a gem of a village in the former county of Westmorland. There a pretty whitewashed cottages either side of two village greens and the river Lowther runs through.

Askham Hall is a 14th century pele tower converted into an Elizabethan mansion in the mid-16th century by Thomas Sandford, whose family lived in it until 1828, when it became a rectory. It has three irregular wings around an oblong courtyard. Askham Hall was the home of Lord Lonsdale since the dismantling of nearby Lowther Castle. It is now a wonderful, upmarket country house hotel.

The area around Askham has been inhabited since the late Stone Age, with two embanked enclosures on nearby Skirsgill Hill, and other prehistoric sites at nearby Moor Divock. There is a bridleway to Moor Divock from Askham.

 ACCOMMODATION & FOOD

* Full details on pages 66 & 68

Askham Hall Kitchen Garden Cafe, Askham, Penrith CA10 2PF
01931 712348 | enquiries@askhamhall.co.uk
askhamhall.co.uk

Askham Hall, Askham, Penrith CA10 2PF
01931 712350 | enquiries@askhamhall.co.uk
askhamhall.co.uk

The George and Dragon, Clifton, nr Penrith CA10 2ER
01768 865381 | enquiries@georgeanddragonclifton.co.uk
georgeanddragonclifton.co.uk

Punchbowl Inn, Askham, Penrith CA10 2PF
01931 712443 | punchbowlinnaskham@gmail.com
punchbowlinnaskham.com

▶ ROUTE DESCRIPTION

Leave the village down the hill, passing the Punchbowl on your right. The road passes over a bridge and then climbs through open parkland past Lowther Church until it reaches Lowther Newtown, built to replace the settlement demolished to build the Castle (visible to your right during the climb) in 1806. Follow the road straight on, then bear left at a diagonal crossroads to reach the A6. Turn left here and after about 50 yards turn right (signs for Melkinthorpe). The road leads downhill and under the railway past Abbott Lodge. A couple of hundred yards further on there is a right turn signposted to Great Strickland. This pretty, but narrow lane leads you into Great Strickland. Turn left down the main street.

GREAT STRICKLAND

In addition to the Strickland Arms (also near Penrith, see page 73), where Sir Bradley Wiggins' 2012 Tour de France yellow jersey may be seen, the village also offers such diverse businesses as web design and picture framing. The church, dedicated to St Barnabas, was built in 1872.

The village still retains its medieval linear design and many of the ancient boundaries can still be seen. It was – and still is – an agricultural village. On the village side of the church is a small walled area with a maple tree. This was the village 'pinfold' where stray cattle or sheep were tethered until their owner retrieved them.

The 17th century Quaker preacher and botanist Thomas Lawson is probably Gt Strickland's most famous son. He ran a local school with an improbably high number of pupils going on to study at Oxford and Cambridge. The old Quaker meeting house was on the site of what is now a bungalow next to the Strickland Arms. There is an abundance of rare flora and fauna in the hedgerows on the Morland road, identified by Cumbria County Council as of 'special' interest.

GREAT STRICKLAND → MORLAND

▶ ROUTE DESCRIPTION

Continue east down the main street towards the Pennines. Local weather lore states that if you can see the Pennines then it's going to rain. If you can't see them it is raining. Leave the village past the church and keep on the road, ignoring a left turn.

There is now a climb,with woods on your right and if riding this stretch at dusk or in the early morning then be aware that deer may suddenly jump out into the road. Past a crossroads the route then begins its descent into Morland

ACCOMMODATION

Strickland Arms, Great Strickland, Penrith, CA10 3DF
Run by: Anton & Penny Flaherty

WILL ORGANISE YOUR TRIP FOR YOU. Famously playing host to Wiggo and Team Sky during the 2012 Tour of Britain, the Arms is going from strength to strength. The new fleece-lined log-built yurt sleeps 10 and there's room for 6 more in the pub. The Arms is on the new C2C route via Ullswater, details of which can be found on the C2C website's Home Page map browser. It's a warm and friendly pub with lots of character, in the heart of Eden Valley, five miles from Penrith. The pub now has Wiggo's yellow jersey from the Tour de France, plus other Team Sky mementos. Real fires, cask ales, a decent selection of wines to go with homemade food cooked by Penny.

Rooms: 2T/D.
Yurt: 10s from £25.
B&B: £30-£45.
Eve meal: £6 - £15.
Pk lunch: Yes - depends what you want.
Secure lock up. Bike washing facility.

01931 712238
stricklandarmspenrith@hotmail.co.uk
thestricklandarms.co.uk

MORLAND

The approach to the village from Great Strickland reveals a vista of modern outskirts, however, the centre of Morland more than makes up for this. Turn right at the (now closed) garage (the church opposite has an Anglo-Saxon tower) and follow the road downhill to the village square, where the Mill Yard Café and Crown pub face each other by the bridge over Morland Beck.

WHERE TO EAT

The Mill Yard Café, The Square, Morland, Penrith CA10 3AZ. Charming converted mill by the bridge in Morland run by Robert and Sarah Kite. Breakfasts, lunches and open some evenings. Home baking, soups, and sandwiches (steak a speciality). Fairtrade tea and coffee. Open 9-5.00 (9-4.00 winter months. Closed Tuesdays). Curry night: last Thursday of every month. RJ's Pizza night every Friday. Saturdays: restaurant night (booking essential).
01931 714155.
info@millyardcafe.co.uk
millyardcafe.co.uk

 ACCOMMODATION

Greengill Bunk Barn, Morland, Cumbria, CA10 3AX

Run by: Freddy Markham

Great spot for cycle groups with two rooms sleeping 16. There is a huge, high-ceiling living room with sofas, table tennis, pool and a splendid music system. Downstairs there is a big kitchen with communal dining table, showers and loos and out the back is a campsite which takes 5 motorhomes or caravans plus 12 tents. A wonderful spot on the edge of a beautiful village where there's a pub and restaurant/tearoom. There are also cottages for rent.

Rooms: 2 sleeping 8 each.
Beds: £240 a night for the whole place.
Camping: £15 per pitch.
£10 for a single pitch.
Secure lock-up for bunk barn.

01931 714244
freddy@greengillholidays.co.uk
greengillholidays.co.uk

 ROUTE DESCRIPTION

Leave Morland down Water Street (turn right at the pub) and follow the road for a mile or so to a crossroads by an electricity substation. Turn left here (signpost to King's Meaburn) and after an undulating ride cross the ford (use the bridge for preference as the concrete of the ford is very slippery) and climb a short and steep hill into King's Meaburn.

KINGS MEABURN

King's Meaburn is a linear village, of Anglo-Saxon origin. Its name, however, derives from the the 12th century, when King Henry II granted part of the area to Sir Hugh de Morville, one of Thomas à Becket's murderers and another part to Sir Hugh's sister, Maud de Veteripont. The King eventually claimed Hugh's land back after the two fell out, hence the name; however, Maud's name lives on in Mauld's Meaburn a few miles to the south.

WHERE TO EAT & DRINK

The White Horse.
Run by Paul and Jessica Fields.
Comfortable whitewashed country pub with open fire. Corby Bitter and an equally well kept selection of guest beers. Seasonal menu of locally sourced home-cooked produce.
Mon-Fri: 5.00-12.00 (Food 6.00-8.00 M, T; 6.00-9.00 T,F,S).
Sat-Sun: 12.00-late (Food Sun 12.00-2.30 and 6.00-8.00).
Pie and Pint Fridays – booking essential.
01931 714256
paul@the-white-horse-in.co.uk.
the-white-horse-in.co.uk

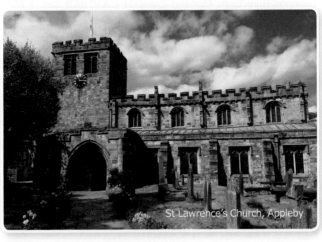
St Lawrence's Church, Appleby

ROUTE DESCRIPTION

Turn south out of King's Meaburn (right at the top of the hill from the ford) and proceed south for approximately two miles, then take a gentle left turn signposted for Colby and Appleby. The road winds and goes up and down, finishing in a descent into Colby. Turn right here and follow the road over the bridge up hill out of the village. Three miles or so later you will find yourself at the eastern end of Appleby in Westmorland, formerly the County town. Turn left and follow the road up past the castle wall to the head of Boroughgate, Appleby's main street.

APPLEBY IN WESTMORLAND

Appleby retains its medieval street pattern, occupying a strategic loop in the River Eden. Boroughgate is the wide main street, leading down past first the High Cross to the Low Cross and the Church of St Lawrence. The only medieval building is the castle, now in private ownership, which stands guard at the top of the hill, Other medieval street names are in evidence, such as Doomgate and Bongate on the other side of the bridge at the bottom of the hill.

The castle passed in the 17th century to the redoubtable Lady Anne Clifford, who took the running of her estates very seriously and restored not only Appleby castle but also that at Brougham near Penrith as well as others at Skipton and Brough. In Appleby she also built the pretty little courtyard of almshouses on the north side of Boroughgate. Notable MPs for Appleby include William Pitt the Younger (very briefly), John Robinson (whose ingenuity and speed at political fixing give us the phrase 'Before you can say Jack Robinson') and Viscount Howick, who as Earl Grey, led the government that passed the great Reform Act of 1832. Several members of George Washington's family attended the Grammar School

Appleby boasts pubs, cafés, a branch of Barclay's Bank and a proper old-fashioned ironmongers. Every June the entire town is taken over by the annual horse fair and if you are proposing to stay here round that time be warned that accommodation is likely to be very scarce and that a form of organised chaos reigns for about a week. In calmer times it is a lovely timeless spot to linger.

TOURIST INFORMATION

Tourist Information Office, the Moot Hall, Boroughgate.
017683 51177
visitcumbria.com/evnp/appleby-tourist-information-centre/

WHERE TO EAT & DRINK

The Crown and Cushion, Boroughgate. Comfortable multi-roomed Robinsons' pub.

The Midland Hotel, 25 Clifford Street. Up a steep hill by the railway station (Settle to Carlisle line). Ingeniously and stylishly refurbished station pub with fine range of real ales and food.

Ruby's, 5a Bridge Street, CA16 6QY. Café and deli with an enterprisingly eclectic menu. Wine and beers available. In the capable hands of young James Brighurst who is keen to welcome cyclists. 017683 51923.

Eden River Cafe, 5 Bridge St, CA16 6QH. Home made cakes, scones, soups, paninis and a good range of coffees and herbal teas. Helen and Dave Sykes run a great resource high in calories and low in price. 017863 54119.

Desi Spice, High Weind. Small, friendly Indian restaurant. Takeaway available. 017683 52368.

Ashiana, 9 Bridge Street. Larger Indian restaurant attracting very good reviews. 017683 53550.

 ## ACCOMMODATION

Tufton Arms Hotel, Market Square, Appleby in Westmorland, Cumbria CA16 6XA
Run by: Nigel Milsom
Upmarket coaching inn combining Victorian elegance with some stylish modern twists. Relaxed and informal, there is a first rate fish restaurant (plus a grill menu for meat eaters) and a lively bar. The Tufton Arms is bang in the town centre, just over the River Eden and close to wonderful Boroughgate, which doesn't look like it's changed for centuries. For the past 25 years, the Milson family has run this friendly place and recently the bedrooms and main dining room have been completely refurbished.
Rooms: 24 - a mixture of T and D.
B&B: from £45
(for best deals go to the website).
Eve meal: mains £7.75 to £14.50
(except for steaks).
Lunch: same.
Pk lunch: Pre-order.
Cycle storage and drying facilities.
017683 51593
info@tuftonarmshotel.co.uk
tuftonarmshotel.co.uk

Bongate House, Bongate, Appleby-in-Westmorland, Cumbria CA16 6UE

Run by: John & Mary Geary

Family run Georgian guest house with huge gardens. Charming and peaceful spot to rest up and just a short stroll into town or to the Royal Oak pub. Hearty breakfast and comfortable rooms, there's free wifi throughout. Hose pipe, tool kits and padlocks for bikes.

Rooms: 8 T/D, 1S. 6 are en-suite.
B&B: from £35.
Eve meal: local pub.
Pk lunch: £5.
Secure lock up and drying facilities.
017683 51245
stay@bongatehouse.co.uk
bongatehouse.co.uk

APPLEBY ▸ BROUGH

▶ ROUTE DESCRIPTION

Leave Appleby by riding to the top of Boroughgate and following the B6260. Just before the hamlet of Burrells, turn left and keep on this road before you turn left again and shortly afterwards once more into Bleatarn. Leave Bleatarn heading north-west and continue into Warcop. Don't be alarmed if you hear the sound of heavy gunfire: there's a large army artillery and tank training range on the slopes of the Pennines north of the village. The village has a church of 12th century origin and a small school. At the time of going to press, the pub, regrettably, remains shut. A short backtrack west on the B6259 (turn left off this where signposted or you will end up on the busy A66) will bring you to Sandford, where the Sandford Arms has fared better.

🍴 WHERE TO EAT & DRINK

The Sandford Arms, Sandford, Appleby, CA16 6NR.
Accommodation available. 017683 51121

121

ACCOMMODATION

The Coach House, Eden Gate, Warcop, Appleby, CA16 6PL

Leave Warcop on the B6259 and enjoy the tranquil pleasures of the middle Eden Valley (less tranquil if there is a firing day on the ranges). Keep straight on when the B6259 dives south and follow Swindale Lane through Great Musgrave and then along the banks of Swindale Beck until it goes under the thundering A66 trans-Pennine route, before turning right on to the main street of Brough.

BROUGH

Brough has always consisted of two distinct settlements: Market Brough to the north and Church Brough, clustered to the south round a green by the church and castle. The division was emphasised in 1977 by the building of the A66 flyover. Brough offers pubs, accommodation, fish and chips and a late-night shop. The farm by the castle has an ice cream parlour.

WHERE TO EAT & DRINK

Bev's Fish and Chips, New Road, Brough, CA17 4AS

Chofh's Tearoom and Takeaway, New Road, Brough, CA17 4AS

The Inn at Brough, Main Street, Brough, Cumbria CA17 4AX..
See next page.

ACCOMMODATION

The Inn at Brough, Main Street, Brough, Cumbria CA17 4AX.

Run by: Sally Coplowe & Jula Coleman
Superbly renovated coaching inn bang on the new route. Top luxury for modest prices (mini fridges, safe and wifi, etc) with extremely comfortable beds. All rooms en-suite. Lively bar serving cask ales. There is a strong local flavour here: the kitchen uses seasonal and local ingredients and the staff are friendly and welcoming. The chef brings with him 2 AA Rosettes experience.

Rooms: 14. 3S, 9 D/T. 2 suites.
B&B: from £55 (two sharing D/T room) to £175 for the top suite.
Eve meal: Bar snacks and à la carte restaurant. Restaurant menu from £13.50 to roughly £27 for a 3-course dinner. Good wine list.
Pk lunch: yes - pse pre-order.
Secure cycle storage, and drying facilities to be offered later in the year.
01768 341252
info@theinnatbrough.co.uk
theinnatbrough.co.uk

Greena, North Stainmore, Kirkby Stephen Cumbria CA17 4EA

Run by: Martin Bell
Comfortable, secure accommodation for rider and bike, 50 yds from Wiggo's Way. Has a double room with en-suite shower in an annexe to the main house, plus two others in the house. Bike washing plus drying room. No evening meal, but transport to and from pub provided on request.

B&B: from £32.50.
Rooms: 3D.
Eve meal: lift to pub available.
Pk lunch: pse pre-order.
Secure lock-up.
01768 342538 / 07921 062179
mhb.greena@gmail.com
bike-stay.net/uk/lodging/england/greena.php

▶ The next stage leads over the Pennines and the last major opportunity to stock up on provisions lies in Kirkby Stephen, five miles south of Brough. There is a wider choice of accommodation here as well, should you wish to make the detour. Unfortunately the cycle shop has closed, but the Pink Geranium café sells inner tubes and there is talk of a cycle hire/repair facility being opened at the very helpful Tourist Information office.

🍴 WHERE TO EAT & DRINK

The King's Arms, Market Street (accommodation available).
Mulberry Cafe

BROUGH → MIDDLETON IN TEESDALE

▶ ROUTE DESCRIPTION

If you have stayed in Kirkby Stephen then head back to Brough and
turn right at the clock. Leave Brough bearing to the north on the
B6276. It is 15 miles to Middleton in Teesdale and the climb up the
flanks of the Pennines, which is a stiff one, begins almost at once.
Behind, there are views over the green Eden Valley almost until the
road reaches and hugs the 1300ft contour. Red flags to the left of
the route on the way up mark the eastern boundary of the ranges at
Warcop and again the early part of the ride may be punctuated by
the sound of artillery fire. This is desolate, exposed country, with the
occasional farm, causing you to appreciate the unforgiving harshness
of making a living up here. After the Co. Durham border sign the
road undulates until moorland gives way to greener scenery and
after skirting two reservoirs, you begin the descent into Middleton
in Teesdale on what has now become the B6277. There is a sign
showing both left and right into Middleton - the left option is easier.

MIDDLETON IN TEESDALE

Middleton in Teesdale is a small, sturdy market town on the north bank of the River Tees. Once more, the early lead and iron ore mining industry was the reason for the settlement's growth and it is said that the co-operative society which was founded here may predate the Rochdale Pioneers. There is still a Co-operative store in Middleton, which also offers hotels, pubs, fish and chips and a bookshop and gives a general air of hardy self-sufficiency.

The Tourist Information Centre is only open in the mornings, but the bookshop over the road is a useful source of information at other times. Once more, your route touches that of Wainwright's Coast to Coast walk, although people doing that will be facing the increasingly bleak approach to the eastern slopes of Cross Fell, to be rewarded at the summit by the prospect of Eden, from which you have just come.

LOCAL INFORMATION

Tourist Information Centre, 10 Market Place, Middleton in Teesdale DL12 0QG
03000 262626
thisisdurham.com/visitor-info/middleton-in-teesdale-visitor-information-point-p113191

ACCOMMODATION

Brunswick House, 55 Market Place, Middleton in Teesdale, Durham, DL12 0QH

Run by: Andrew Milnes

Rooms reflect the many period features of the house such as Georgian fireplaces and exposed beams, whilst being fully up to date for comfort. Egyptian cotton bedding and rooms have mini fridge, tv/dvd player and wifi. The cosy lounge has a log fire. Visit Britain 4 star rating plus a Silver Award and a Breakfast award. Members of the ETC cyclists and walkers welcome scheme. Lovely local produce available for evening meals.

Rooms: 3D, 2T.
B&B: £40 (£50 single occ going up to £60 in Jan).
Eve meal: £20 for 2-courses, £24 for 3.
Pk lunch: £5.
Secure cycle storage and lock-up.

01833 640393
enquiries@brunswickhouse.net
brunswickhouse.net

The Forresters Hotel & Restaurant,
52/53 Market Place, Middleton,
DL12 0QH
Run by: Franck Marie

Superb little hotel right in the middle of
Middleton, run by a French couple. Needless
to say, the food is excellent (Mme Marie
does the cooking and brings to Teesdale a flavour
of her native Normandy). Ice cream, desserts and chocolates all
made by Mme Marie. Light lunches possible and the breakfast menu
ranges from pancakes and Breakfast Gateau to the full Monty English.
Freeview TV and wifi in rooms. Bar serves cocktails, real ale, wines by
the glass and has a pool table. A splendid new addition with a large
terrace.
Rooms: 3T, 3D, 2S.
B&B: from £35 (£45 single occ).
Lunch: 2 courses for £9.95 or baguettes and wraps.
Eve meal: starters £4.95 to £8.50, mains £9.95 to £20.95.
Weekend lunches: £12.95 for 2 courses, £15.95 for 3.
Bar meals and snacks also available.
Secure cycle lock-up and drying facilities.
01833 641435
info@forrestersmiddleton.co.uk
forrestersmiddleton.com

MIDDLETON IN TEESDALE → STANHOPE

▶ ROUTE DESCRIPTION

Leave Middleton on the B6262 and follow it to Eggleston, where
you turn left and north on to the B6278. Eggleston is mentioned in
12th century tax records and the remains of the medieval ridge and
furrrow field patterns can still be seen. Once again it was lead mining
that put Eggleston on the map. Exit the village over Blackton Beck,
where there is a sharp dog-leg. The road heads north on a terrace
in the contours and is unfenced for a fair bit of the way. Abandoned
mineworkings can be seen on the moor, but investigating them is not
advised. After a carpark, where the road bends left it begins to climb
again before beginning its descent across Bollihope Common. Be
warned that there is a sharp bend at the bottom of the valley where
the road crosses Bollihope Burn. After this there is one more ascent
before it drops into Stanhope to rejoin the main C2C (finishing very
steeply). It is better to turn left at the ford and cross the Wear by the
bridge upstream.

STANHOPE ← Full details on page 106-109

FROSTERLEY & WOLSINGHAM

With numbers on the route increasing every year there are accommodation bottlenecks so you might wish to look at the options here. As for getting back onto the route, you can either retrace your steps to Stanhope or take your life into your hands and cut up country to the A68, linking up with the C2C at Castleside. St Godric once lived in this Saxon settlement with Elric the Hermit, around 1120.

Wolsingham sits at the confluence of the River Wear and Waskerley Beck. It is a Saxon settlement and one of the first market towns in County Durham, deriving its name from Waelsingas (sons of Wael, an ancient Saxon family that once resided there). The earliest known record of the town is to be found in Reginald of Durham's Life of Godric. Once upon a time everyone owed their living to the Prince Bishop. There was a thriving population of shepherds, plough-makers, beekeepers, forest keepers, wood turners, carters etc.

 ACCOMMODATION

Black Bull, 27 Market Place, Wolsingham, Co Durham DL13 3AB

Run by: Linda Bell & Billy Sloan

Under the new ownership of cycling enthusiasts Linda and Billy, this characterful town centre pub has been completely refurbished and now has a family room which sleeps six. Good ale and hearty food, from soup and baguettes to steak and mixed grills, all home-cooked. There's a lock-up round the back, plus tool kit and the rooms are comfortable and inexpensive. The new couple are keen to encourage cycling and offer a warm welcome.

Rooms: 1F (sleeps 6), 2D/T

B&B: from £15 for family room if fully occupied (£90) or £32.50 for sharing D/T.

Eve meal: yes.

Pk lunch: pre-order.

Secure cycle lock-up. Drying facilities.

01388 527332 / 07752 580309

info@blackbullwolsingham.co.uk

blackbullwolsingham.co.uk

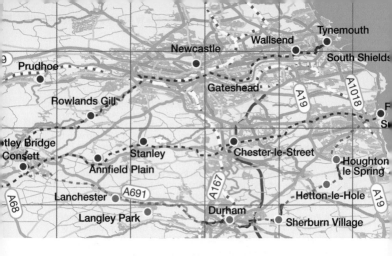

HOWNSGILL→DURHAM→SUNDERLAND

**This braid was added last year as an alternative end to
the ride, taking in historic Durham and the scenic village
of Lanchester. It links up with the W2W route at Durham,
winding its way up to Sunderland.**

Lanchester dates from Roman times, when there was a fort with
1,000 soldiers on Dere Street, the great road connecting York and
Corbridge. Its drift mine closed in the 1970s and now the place is
a pretty residential village with close connections to farming.

- Shortly after crossing the A68 at Castleside you will come to Hownsgill
Viaduct, a magnificent creation of the steam age, with splendid views
across the north east. Immediately after the mighty bridge comes
Lydgetts Junction, where you should turn right onto Route 14, marked
Lanchester and Durham.

- The route follows the old railway line past Knitsley Farm with its shop
(worth a stop). Lanchester is about 4 miles away, and is a pleasant
market village with three pubs, a deli and a small shopping centre.

- It is a further eight miles to Durham, mostly following the same
disused rail track, passing Langley Park and Bearpark before coming
to Baxter Woods on the outskirts of the city.

- Turn right onto Toll House Rd and just past Neville Dene turn left into Monica Grove and right onto Redhills Lane then take the next (sharp) right into Sutton Place. Take the next sharp left onto the A690 and then the traffic free section which takes you to Milburngate Bridge, where instead of crossing you briefly follow Framwellgate before crossing at the next bridge, then back to Leazes Rd (the other side of the Milburngate Bridge).

- You will shortly be on traffic-free path again which takes you down to the River Wear where you turn left before passing Baths Bridge. Follow the river with Pelaw Wood on your left. Where the river bears to the right the path will now part company with the Wear, going through Old Durham to Bent House Lane, where you head left.

- Follow NCN 14 along Renny's Lane and over the A1M, where it becomes a traffic free path again. Follow 14 into Sherburn, following Dowsey Rd then left at the T-junction into Lady's Place Lane onto Regional Route 20, passing to the west of Low Pittington. Keep on Route 20.

  It soon becomes traffic free. Continue following Route 20 through Hetton-le-Hole and left onto the Great Northern Forest Trail, crossing the B1404 and then over the A19. There's a sharp left along a traffic free section alongside the A19 before RR20 heads right through East Herrington and then Farringdon.

- Keep to the left of the ornamental lake (though you can equally follow the other path to the right) and you will shortly link up with NCN1 which presently takes you to Sunderland's famous Wearmouth Bridge. Take the cycle lane over the bridge and link up with the end of the C2C, through to Roker.

Durham: possibly the finest stop-off point along the route. Work on the cathedral started almost a millennium before the Millennium Dome. For more information: **thisisdurham.com.** Let us know of cycle friendly accommodation in this tiny gem of a city. Feedback would be much appreciated.

WASKERLEY WAY

A Potted History
Formerly part of the old railway from Rookhope to Consett the path has been converted into an excellent traffic free route for walkers and cyclists.

PLACES OF INTEREST

Hownsgill Viaduct - located at mile marker 108.6 this very impressive 150 foot high bridge almost dares you to look down into the gorge and not feel dizzy!

Parkhead Station -Terry and Lorraine Turnbull - tel: 01388 526434 - Tea Rooms offering wholesome home made food, snacks, sandwiches and evening meals. Open all year - if there is nobody about just knock!

CASTLESIDE

Castleside sits either side of the A68 high up on the Durham moors and leads down to Consett via Moorside. Close to the Hownsgill viaduct, it marks the approach of the great industrial hinterland that boomed throughout the industrial revolution before the smelters and pits closed down in the 1980s.

ACCOMMODATION

Bee Cottage Guesthouse, Castleside, Consett
Co. Durham, DH8 9HW
Run by: David Blackburn & Irene Mordey
One of the favoured watering holes of seasoned C2Cers, Bee Cottage is a 4-star licensed guesthouse with stunning views across Co Durham. On a bend in the Waskerley Way just beyond Park Head Plantation, it is on the edge of a pretty little coppice at Redhouse Farm, a couple of miles before the A68 at Castleside. Warm welcome. You can eat, drink and sleep soundly here - a 'one-stop-shop.' New this year: a light meals and snacks menu plus barbecue and buffet on weekends. Member of the Walkers & Cyclists Welcome schemes. New flat screen TVs and lots of improvements. Wifi throughout.
Rooms: 2D, 2T, 4F (8 en-suite).
B&B: from £35-£40. £10 single supplement.
Eve meal: 3-courses £20. Alcohol licence.
Pk lunch: yes.
Secure cycle storage.
Distance from route: 400 metres.
Visit Britain 4-star & Cyclists Welcome Scheme.
Drying facilities.
01207 508224
beecottage68@aol.com
beecottage.co.uk

Deneview, 15 Front Street, Castleside, Consett, DH8 9AR

Run by: Catherine O'Keefe

Superior B & B accommodation in Castleside village. Colour digital TV. Radio and Tea/Coffee making facilities. Only 25 yards from an excellent pub serving meals each day. 4 Diamond Award.

Rooms: 1D, 1T, 2S (all en-suite).
B&B: £32.50-£40.
Eve meal: local pub (25 metres).
On route. 4-star. Secure cycle parking.
01207 502925
catherine@deneview.co.uk
deneview.co.uk

The Manor House Inn, Carterway Heads, Northumbria DH8 9LX

Run by: Chris Baxter

Food served all day here, great local real ales plus accommodation at this excellent new addition to the guide, bang on the Muggleswick Common alternative to Waskerley Way. Just 4 miles from Castleside and Shotley Bridge, ideal for road bikes avoiding the off-road section from Parkhead to Consett. 18th century coaching inn with picnic terrace overlooking the Derwent Valley. Local produce includes game and wild fish and food comes highly recommended, from bar snacks to à la carte.

Rooms: 4D/T, 1F.
B&B: £37.50. **Single occ:** £55
Eve meal: bar and restaurant
(mains from around £10).
Pk lunch: yes.
Secure lock-up and drying facilities.
01207 255268
themanorhouseinn@gmail.com
themanorhouseinn.com

CONSETT

Whether you are coming via Edmundbyers Common or Stanhope, you will shortly be passing the 100 mile point stamping station at the Bike Stop at the start of the Waskerley Way. You can get spares and repairs here, or tea and cake. And it's all down hill from here.

This is a pleasant and easy section of the route, past Muggleswick Common, Waskerley and Smiddy Shaw reservoirs, followed by a quick canter into Park Head Plantation near Bee Cottage, and down to the A68. Beyond here is the magnificent Hownsgill Viaduct, which carried the Stanhope and Tyne Railway Line, Britain's first private commercial railway route. There are great views from here across sweeping tracts of deciduous forest and undulating landscape, on the edge of an area that was once the embodiment of heavy British industry.

The pathway is dotted with imaginative Sustrans signage and sculptures cast from industrial relics. Just before Consett are the Terris Novalis sculptures, which overlook the 700-acre site of what was once the mighty Consett Steelworks. The Turner prize winning works - a stainless steel theodolite and an engineer's level by Tony Cragg - are nearly 7m tall, are 20 times life size, and symbolise regeneration in an area convulsed by the death of heavy industry towards the end of the last century. The art works were commissioned by Sustrans and will stand as a monument to this admirable body long after the combustion engine has coughed its last.

PLACES OF INTEREST

Phileas Fogg - alias Derwent Valley Foods Factory. You will smell it before you see it. Shotley Bridge is an old spa town, well-known for German sword-makers in the 17th century.

C2C Features - dotted along the line are story-boards set on vertical sleepers which interpret the history of the railway. These are chapters taken from a novel, The Celestial Railroad, by John Downie.

◎ CYCLE SHOPS

Consett Cycle Co, 62 Medomsley Rd 01207 581205

USEFUL SERVICES

The Bike Bus, The Bus Station, Stanley, Co Durham DH9 0NQ

Cyclist and bike transport specialists. Transport throughout the UK and size of group no object. Very competitive rates. For more details, see ad on inside back cover.

01207 230000 or Durham 0191 383 2905

stanleytaxis.co.uk

bike.bus@btconnect.com

▶ DIRECTIONS

- At Consett the routes part company for the final time; one goes to Sunderland and the other to Newcastle. The split in the route comes just after the Hownsgill Viaduct. On the other side of the lane the route either goes straight on through the centre of Consett to Sunderland. Or you can turn left for Newcastle and Tynemouth. If you go left you will pass the outskirts of Shotley Bridge, whose centre is surprisingly pretty, and then on along the Derwent Walk to Rowlands Gill. I will deal with that later, but for the moment will describe the original route as it progresses gently and scenically into Sunderland. From Consett you head for Stanley, but first you have to get out of Consett, so pay heed to the signs.

- Go round the A692 roundabout, briefly up the left side of Front St before going left between Edith Street and Albert Rd. Cross the latter half way up and go right into Park Rd, cross Front St before heading left and across the B6308, then the path takes you through Leadgate and past the Annfield Plain. Look out for the Kyo Undercurrents sculpture - a series of earth and stone ramps.

 WHERE TO EAT

Maddisons, 26 Front St, Consett DH8 5AQ

Run by: Heather Price

Independent 'drinks house & eatery' where, quite apart from fresh squeezed juices, splendid wines, cocktails and craft beers, you can eat delicious home baked breads, cakes, pastries and scones. Food ranges from £1.95 for cakes to £7.95 for an all-out Geordie breakfast burger. There is also Reuben Northern Style (homemade Yorkshire pudding filled with pastrami and mustard gravy), Croque Maddison (toasted organic white or wholemeal pulled ham sandwich topped with welsh rarebit: £4.95) and a toothsome flatbread with balsamic beetroot, red onion, feta, pomegranate and rocket (£5.95).

They have a repertoire of 450 different scones! And any sort of sandwich you could think of. A great resource well worth taking the trouble to find.

Open: 7 days a week 9-5.
Secure cycle storage.

01207 583318
heatherprice0@gmail.com
maddisonsconsett.co.uk

Jolly Drovers Pub, Leadgate, Consett, DH8 6RR.

New lease of life breathed into this pub on the route, with great food now served all day. The new owners have spent a lot of time and money and getting the Drovers just right and now there is a combination of bar food and restaurant fare, plus all manner of drinks. Bike rack outside. Ideal fuel-stop before the final stretch.

01207 500999

ACCOMMODATION

Consett YMCA, Parliament St, Consett, Co. Durham, DH8 5DH

Run by: Terry Page

There is a drying room, workshop for repairs, colour TV, bar and lounge, pool table, and even a gym if you have the energy left! Ideal for large groups, accommodating up to 45 people. Consett YMCA also organises lots of outdoor activities. Adventure Activities Programmes and holidays a speciality.

Rooms: 10 multi-occ.
Bed only: £15.
B&B: £21.
Eve Meal: £7.
Pk lunch: £4.
01207 502680
ymca@derwentside.org.uk
consettymca.org

Crown and Crossed Swords Hotel, Front Street, Shotley Bridge, Consett, Co. Durham, DH8 0HU

Run by: Sheila, Victoria or Maureen

Vibrant pub in the heart of the scenic village of Shotley Bridge, a short hop from the Consett-Rowlands Gill route. Lovely old fashioned public bar with coal fire and well kept real ale. There's also a lounge bar, restaurant and ten letting rooms. Private car park. Time has stood still here. But no-one stands still in the new and popular Swordmaker's Restaurant, with its home-cooked traditional dishes.

Open Mon-Fri 4-9pm; Sat 12-9pm; Sun 12-3pm

Rooms: 1S, 2D, 4T, 3F (4 en-suite).

B&B: from £25. Single occ. £30.

Eve meal: Swordmaker's Restaurant (closed Sunday night).

Pk lunch: please book in advance.

Distance from route: 500 metres.

Ideal for groups (up to 21). Secure cycle parking.

01207 502006

a1tourism.com/uk/crown4.html

STANLEY & BEAMISH

Stanley is set on a breezy hilltop and commands a bird's eye view of the whole area. A former mining town situated between Consett and Chester-le-Street, the name comes from Anglo-Saxon and means 'stony field'. It was first mentioned in 1211 and there are Neolithic and Roman remains in the area.

ACCOMMODATION

Bobby Shafto Caravan Park

Run by: Andrew Peel

10-acre caravan and camping park just beyond the Beamish Museum where you can camp or stay in a camping pod or simply book a caravan for the night (NB for hire vans please bring your own linen)). There's an on site bar and pool room and facilities include a centrally heated amenity building with showers etc, plus a shop. A pretty self-contained site, but within easy distance of pubs and eateries.

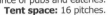
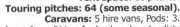

Tent space: 16 pitches.

Touring pitches: 64 (some seasonal).

Caravans: 5 hire vans, Pods: 3.

Prices: from £11pp for backpackers/cyclists (£13 high season) .

Tent with 2 or more people or motorcar, touring caravan or campervan: £22 (£27 high season).

Pods can be booked for 1 night or more.

Caravans for hire: from £42 per night per caravan - minimum booking is 3 nights.

Those booking online should quote reference: **C2C15**.

0191 370 1776

info@bobbyshaftocaravanpark.co.uk

bobbyshaftocaravanpark.co.uk

Beamish Mary Inn, No Place, Stanley, Durham DH9 0QH

Run by: Sally Crowther

Splendid old-fashioned pub with lots of quirky charm, now famous thanks to the TV series George Gently (Martin Shaw), it's a perfect last night watering-hole and ideal for small groups. Great beers (8 real ales). And a 3-course meal for only £14.95. It is such a delight to see a perfectly preserved old inn that time has somehow passed by.

B&B: from £22.50 (if sharing family room) to £35.
Rooms: 1D, 1T/D, 1F (sleeps 4).
Eve meal: £14.95 for 3-courses.
Pk lunch: pse pre-order.
Secure cycle storage and drying facilities.
0191 370 0237
info@beamishmaryinn.co.uk
beamishmaryinn.co.uk

South Causey Inn, Beamish Burn Rd, Stanley, Co Durham DH9 0LS

Run by: Susan & Philip Moiser

An ideal last night stop-off, ideal for groups. Food is served from breakfast time until 9pm (8.30pm Sundays) and ranges from bar snacks to full à la carte (around £28 for three filling and wholesome courses). Winner of Tourism Pub of the Year (Visit England) for the North East and Scotland, plus National winner of the Great British Pub Awards Family Pub of the Year. A really professional outlet in a part of the world not blessed for this. Real ales and a good wine list.. Jacuzzi baths and hot tubs in some rooms, and private dining possible for cycling groups. Dog friendly.

Rooms: 29.
B&B: from £42pppn.
Eve meal: yes - bar snacks to full à la carte.
Pk lunch: full picnics available.
Secure cycle storage
Drying facilities.
01207 235555
southcausey@hotmail.com
southcausey.co.uk

PLACES OF INTEREST

Beamish Museum is England's largest open-air museum and has a working steam railway, trams, an Edwardian town centre, a demonstration colliery, a school and a working farm. The C2C route passes within yards of the entrance gate. 0191 370 4000.

Tanfield Railway is the oldest railway in the world that still exists. It stops at the Causey Arch north of Stanley - 50m high and a Scheduled Ancient Monument built in 1728 - and is manned by volunteers 0191 274 2002.

Jolly Drovers Maze is built on the site of the former Eden Pit Colliery in 1989. Like the Lambton Worm (see Chester-le-Street) it was designed by Andy Goldsworthy.

STANLEY → SUNDERLAND

16 miles (14 miles traffic-free)

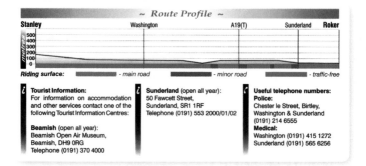

~ Route Profile ~

| Stanley | Washington | A19(T) | Sunderland | Roker |

Riding surface: ▬ - main road ▬ - minor road ▬ - traffic-free

ℹ Tourist Information:
For information on accommodation and other services contact one of the following Tourist Information Centres:

Beamish (open all year):
Beamish Open Air Museum,
Beamish, DH9 0RG
Telephone (0191) 370 4000

ℹ Sunderland (open all year):
50 Fawcett Street,
Sunderland, SR1 1RF
Telephone (0191) 553 2000/01/02

ℹ Useful telephone numbers:
Police:
Chester le Street, Birtley,
Washington & Sunderland
(0191) 214 6555
Medical:
Washington (0191) 415 1272
Sunderland (0191) 565 6256

CHESTER-LE-STREET

▶ DIRECTIONS

- Just follow the transformed transformers (great steel monoliths sculpted from reclaimed scraps known as the Stanley Sphinxes). Don't forget to look at the amazing metal cows near Beamish. Created by Sally Matthews, they are surprisingly graceful as they stand beside the path, turning grass into rust whilst themselves slowly melding into the landscape.

- There's also King Coal by artist David Kemp, next to the abandoned railway line at Pelton Fell. This was built of stone from the dismantled Consett railway station bridge and bricks from old kilns, while British Coal provided the crown. It was put together by a stonemason and local volunteers and was, by sheer coincidence, finished on October 15 1992 - the very day of the announcement of the closure of the last pits in Durham's once booming coalfields.

- Chester-le-Street is the oldest town in County Durham, and was once a Roman settlement. The Washington Wildfowl and Wetlands Centre is very near the route. This 100-acre waterfowl park designed by Peter Scott has over 1,200 birds and is visited by several mammals, including the scarce water vole.

POI

The Washington Wetlands Trust 100 acres of magnificent parkland, ponds and hides.
0191 416 5454

 FOOD

THE WHEATSHEAF PELAW GRANGE
0191 388 3104

THE BARLEY MOW
Browns Buildings
0191 410 4504

 **CYCLE SHOPS**

Cestria Cycles 11 Ashfield Terrace - 0191 388 7535

THE LAMBTON WORM

If you manage to leave the river here in one piece, be thankful! For this is where the Lambton Worm resides (and we are not referring here to the erstwhile politician). The legend runs that a young Lambton lad, fishing in the river against all advice, caught a small worm. In disgust he threw it into a nearby well and went off to fight in the Crusades. On his return the 'worm' had grown into a dragon which ravaged the countryside. A witch agreed to slay the beast on condition that Lambton kill the first living thing he met. Unfortunately it was his father, who of course he spared, and so failed to fulfil his side of the bargain, thus nine generations of Lambtons were condemned to meet untimely ends.

C2C Features: the **Penshaw Monument**, a look-alike Doric Temple dedicated to Theseus, was built in memory of John George Lambton, the 1st Earl of Durham.

Sunderland

▶ DIRECTIONS

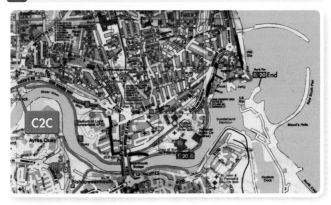

The home run

The last leg of the route is scenic as it follows the north bank of the Wear, skirting Washington and passing the Stadium of Light. This route opened in 2000 and is reasonably easy to follow. The end is near the Marina at Roker, a grand spot to finish. Tradition has it that you dip your wheel in the briny - just as you did at the start.

The River Wear

The River Wear in Sunderland is estuarial, much of it protected for wildlife species and habitat including salt marsh. In the summer it is possible to spot salmon, as well as feeding kittiwakes, common terns, cormorants and herons. Much of the riverside is unrecognisable compared to just 20 years ago when it was dominated by collieries, engineering works and dozens of shipyards. The C2C heads eastwards under the Leamside railway line, which crosses the River Wear via the Victoria Viaduct, so named because it was completed on the day of Queen Victoria's coronation in 1838. The elegant design is based upon a Roman viaduct at Alacantra in Spain.

To mark the official end of the C2C 17 years after the route opened, Sunderland City Council officially unveiled a brand new sculpture (above) by local artist Andrew Small. It was the final piece of his triptych of Wearside statues. His work culminates in a giant letter 'O' at Roker marina, and is designed to frame Roker Pier lighthouse for finish line photo portraits of the many thousands who finish the ride every year.

ABOUT THE CITY

Heritage, history and culture at your seaside rendezvous

Sunderland was once home of shipbuilding, coal-mining, glass blowing and rope making, but it has reinvented itself since becoming a city in 1992, and is now a fascinating mixture of history, heritage and modern facilities to welcome the rider on the last few miles of their voyage. It lies alongside the River Wear, and there has been a major trading hub here since Anglo-Saxon times, when it was one of Europe's major centres of learning and education thanks to the twin monastic settlements of St Peter's (built in 674 with examples of the oldest stained glass in England) and St Paul's. This is where the Venerable Bede wrote the first history of England and it was also here that the art of glass blowing was introduced. By the middle ages, it was one of the biggest and wealthiest towns in England; and that was before the real boom times arrived during the Industrial Revolution, when its population exploded from 15,000 to 150,000 in just a few years. That was when the harbour, created to handle a few small fishing vessels, blossomed into

the biggest international centre for shipbuilding, with as many as 16 working yards. Then, in 1988, more than 550 years of history ended when the last shipyard closed. The coal trains and the heavy industry are long gone, but the grandeur of those Victorian riches can still be seen in echoes of the shipyards visible from the Wearmouth bridge; the elegant architecture, and the city parks at Roker and Mowbray. Now, the dockside that was once filled with soot, coal dust and the sparks flying from the yards, is an elegant sculpture trail where tranquillity and works of art have replaced the thunder of heavy industry. Nowadays, it is a city in tune with nature. The country parks at Herrington and Hetton Lyons are worth the diversion and the route skirts the Wildfowl and Wetland Trust nature reserve at Washington. When you reach the sea you are greeted by the longest stretch of

cityside beach in the UK. Sunderland is also reinventing itself as a modern waterfront city, with bars, restaurants and a thriving nightlife (if you've got the energy for dancing after pedalling over the spine of England) to welcome you. On the way you pass Washington village, the ancestral home of George Washington, winner of the American War of Independence: symbolically completing the loop since Whitehaven, the start of the C2C, is where his grandparents had their home.

🔭 PLACES OF INTEREST

Arts Centre Washington Biddick Lane, Fatfield District 7, Washington, Tyne & Wear, NE38 8AB The Arts Centre Washington is a vibrant focus for arts activities offering a year round programme of arts activities includes exhibitions, theatre, dance, music, festivals, classes and workshops for all ages.
0191 219 3455
artscentrewashington.co.uk

SIGHTS ON YOUR WAY

Riverside Sculpture Trail
Between the Wearmouth Bridge and the Marina, the promenade offers a connected trail of specially commissioned artworks in metal and stone that refer back to the city's history and heritage.

Washington Wildfowl & Wetland Centre
Pattinson, Washington NE38 8LE.
This recreated wetland provides a 'stop over' and wintering habitat for migratory waterbirds after their passage over the North Sea and the Wetland Discovery Centre offers both a window on the wide range of wildlife and a programme of art exhibitions.
0191 416 5454
wwt.org.uk/wetland-centres/washington/

Sunderland Museum & Winter Gardens
Burdon Road, Sunderland SR1 1PP.
Sunderland's museum is hugely popular with visitors of all ages and offers a range of fascinating multimedia installations to tell the city's story from its early foundations to the present day and one of the galleries boasts an extensive collection of paintings by LS Lowry.
0191 553 2323
twmuseums.org.uk

Stadium of Light, SR5 1SU.
Magnificent 48,000-seater stadium built on the site of Wearmouth Colliery which closed in 1994. Well worth a visit, tours are available. Alongside is the brand new Olympic standard 50 metre swimming pool, the only one of its kind between Leeds and Edinburgh.
0191 551 5055
safc.com

The Sunderland Empire
High Street West, Sunderland SR1 3EX.
Opened in 1907, is the North East's largest theatre and a splendid
example of Edwardian architecture. Following a £4.5 million
refurbishment the Empire now boasts 21st Century facilities and is the
only theatre between Manchester and Edinburgh capable of staging
large West End productions.
0870 602 1130 | livenation.co.uk/Sunderland

National Glass Centre
Liberty Way, Sunderland SR6 0GL. Housed in an innovative glass-
roofed building on the north bank of the Wear, the National Glass
Centre is a fascinating experience and visitors can explore the full
history of glass making in the UK and see cutting edge examples of
the contemporary glass maker's art.
0191 515 5555 | nationalglasscentre.com

Northeast Aircraft Museum
This new attraction comes just after the Wetland Centre, near the
Nissan plant and the riverside. The museum is slowly absorbing the
military vehicle collection from the old Newcastle museum and at time
of going to press a mock World War II street was being erected.
nelsam.org.uk

Wearmouth Bridge
Built in 1796 and seen as a catalyst for the growth of Sunderland. The
previous bridge was at Chester-le-Street. There was a pedestrian toll
until 1846, and for vehicles until 1885. The adjacent railway bridge
opened in 1879 and carries both Metro and conventional rail.

Marine Activities Centre
North Dock, Roker, Sunderland SR6 0PW. The marina at Roker is
Sunderland's main focus for all types of water-based sports and
leisure activities and boasts an Italian restaurant with panoramic sea
views. It's also near your C2C finishing line. 0191 514 1847 86

City Centre
Across the Wearmouth Bridge stands Sunderland City Centre,
incorporating great places to eat, drink and shop and includes bike
shops, the Central Railway Station and venues well worth a visit.

St Peter's Church
East of the Wearmouth Bridge,
alongside the C2C and the University
is St Peter's church, home to the
Venerable Bede until he moved to
St Paul's in Jarrow. There is now a
walkway and cycleway linking the two,
and you may spot the small blue signs
for it along the rest of the route.

Sunniside & Sunniside Gardens

A large area of public open space in the eastern part of the city centre. The surrounding area is emerging as a cultural quarter with new bars and restaurants and over 100 listed buildings.

Roker Beach and Pier

With its distinctive red and white granite lighthouse, Roker beach provides a wonderful seaside playground and is an ideal place for water sports, with the Marine Activities Centre and other facilities close by.

WHERE TO EAT & DRINK

There are a number of public houses near the C2C finishing point. The Harbour View, The New Derby, The Cliff, The Queen Vic, the bar of the Roker Hotel and a few others are all within walking distance. The Smugglers, on the promenade at Roker Beach, was voted the top music venue in Sunderland and they have live music most days of the week. Bar meals are available at most of these pubs. There are also a number of excellent Italians in Little Italy on the promenade and Santini's and Gabriele's by the Marriott. For snacks, try the Bungalow Café on the cliff top at Roker. It is a well-known landmark, an old-fashioned cafe in a tiny bungalow. Next to it is the famous signpost, marked: 'To Beach' (pointing towards the beach), 'To Village' (pointing into Roker), 'To Bungalow' (pointing to the cafe), and 'To Germany' (pointing out to sea).

SHAGORIKA traditional Indian, reliable feast.

KING'S ARMS, 1 Beach St, Hanover Place, SR4 6BU. (off Trimdon St behind the B&Q) This is worth the diversion as it's one of the best beer pubs in the North East. It's a ten minute walk from the city centre and is close to the university. Regulars include Timothy Taylor Landlord plus a wide choice of guest beers. There are nine handpumps. Camra pub of the year 2005, 2006 and regional North East winner. Lots of wood panelling, a small snug and lots of pictures of old Sunderland . 0191 567 9804.

SALTGRASS, Hanover Place, SR4 6BY. Quite why two of Sunderland's best ale houses happen to be tucked behind B&Q just south of the Alexandra Bridge is a mystery that will resolve itself after a pint or two of the many guest beers. Old fashioned and friendly. Beamed ceilings, lots of old pictures. Popular for Sunday lunch. 0191 565 7229.

ROKER PIER

MARINA VISTA At the Marina.

ROKER HOTEL TAVISTOCK Thai and Italian.

THROWING STONES Top quality food at the Glass Centre.

THE PROMENADE, Queen's Parade, SR6 8DA Serves
Caledonian, Deuchars and Tetley. Seafront pub with
excellent views. Serves good pub grub and upstairs there
are four single rooms and three twins. 0191 529 2226.

HARBOUR VIEW, Benedict Rd, SR6 0NL Good range
of beers very well kept. As the pub's name suggests,
it has commanding views over the marina and harbour
and is a short distance from Roker beach. Specialises in
microbreweries from near and far and there's a quiz night
Tuesdays and live music on Thursdays. 0191 567 1402.

Photo by Pam Tate.

CYCLE SHOPS

Cycle World, 222 High Street West, Sunderland, SR1 1TZ
0191 5658188 or 5141974, cycleworldshop.co.uk

Peter Darke Cycles, 1/2 John Street, Sunderland, SR1 1DX
0191 5108155, darkecycles.com

Halfords Bike Hut, Unit 3, Trimdon Street, Sunderland, SR4
6DW. 0191 5140843, halfords.com

WHAT NEXT?

Up the coast to join the Reivers route back to the west

There is a wonderful eight mile stretch of coastal ride between Roker
and South Shields, going through Whitburn and Marsden.
Known as the Two Rivers Cycleway, this is part of National Route 1,
which becomes the Coast and Castles route once across the Tyne,
wending a spectacular and beautiful thread up the Northumberland
coast and into the Scottish Borders.

It is also the connection between the C2C and Reivers routes,
completing the full circle in about 330 miles. This route follows the
beautiful beaches on Roker and Seaburn before passing the Souter
Lighthouse and Marsden Rock, descending to the old ferry link. Close
to the Shields' ferry are a number of great bars overlooking the active
Tyne estuary, including the Alum House and bars around Mill Dam /
Custom House.

If you finish in Sunderland but your car or train are from Newcastle,
the Two Rivers Cycleway is the obvious route. Once at South Shields
you have the option of taking the ferry across or taking the pedestrian
and cyclists' tunnel (note: do NOT attempt the car tunnel). Also note:
the Metro does not allow bicycles, though mainline trains do.

Reivers route starts on page 156 ➜

ROWLANDS GILL → TYNEMOUTH

19 miles (17 miles traffic-free)

~ Route Profile ~

| Rowlands Gill | River Tyne | Newcastle upon Tyne | Wallsend | Tyne Tunnel | Tynemouth |

```
500
400
300    metres
200
100
0
```

Riding surface: ▬▬▬ - main road   ▬▬▬ - minor road   ▬▬▬ - traffic-free

i **Tourist Information:**
For information on accommodation and other services contact one of the following Tourist Information Centres:

Gateshead (open all year):
Central Library, Prince Consort Road, Gateshead, NE8 4LN
Telephone (0191) 477 3339

i **Newcastle** (open all year):
Central Exchange Buildings, 132 Grainger Street, Newcastle upon Tyne, NE1 5AF
Telephone (0191) 277 8000

✆ **Useful telephone numbers:**
Police:
Newcastle, North Shields & South Shields (0191) 214 6555
Medical:
Newcastle General Hospital (0191) 273 8811
Queen Elizabeth Hospital, Gateshead (0191) 482 0000

NEWCASTLE

Scenic ride to the Toon

The Newcastle route follows the Derwent Walk. This is both scenic and easy to ride, taking you through Hamsterley Mill, Rowlands Gill and through some pretty landscaped areas alongside the river Derwent. When you get to the Tyne go left and over the bridge to the Hadrian's Way path. Although you start off in a rather unpleasant industrial stretch, you are soon back beside the river.

The ride along the Quayside is one of the high points for me. It follows the start of the Coast & Castles route, and the description which follows borrows heavily from my guide book to that magnificent ride from Newcastle to Edinburgh (Coast & Castles - The Complete Guide). I make no apologies.

Newcastle is one of the most happening places in northern Europe (never mind England). A magnet for shoppers and clubbers, diners and drinkers, it boasts some of Britain's finest architecture and has gone through a cultural Renaissance. Recent restoration projects have included Norman fortifications, 16th century merchant houses and the great neo-classical designs of Grainger Town. There are also art galleries, museums and concert venues aplenty.

Newcastle and Gateshead, its neighbour on the south bank of the Tyne, have been voted England's best short break destination. The two towns also teamed up to contend for the European Capital of Culture in 2008, a link symbolised by the arcing strand of the Gateshead Millennium Bridge across the Tyne. Sadly, the gong went to a town arguably in greater need of culture: Liverpool.

Ever since the Romans arrived 2,000 years ago Newcastle has been a hub of trading activity. The city grew up around Pons Aelius, a Roman fortification about 10 miles inland from the North Sea. For the last 800 years a booming trade in wool, leather and coal have brought the city prosperity.

147

There are now art galleries, museums and concert venues, among them the magnificent Baltic Centre for Contemporary Art on the banks of the Tyne. Of 1930s Art Deco design, the redesignation of this former grain warehouse is typical of the vision and flair that has gone into the area's regeneration.

🔭 POINTS OF INTEREST

CASTLE KEEP, Castle Garth, St Nicholas St. Built by Henry II between 1168-78 on the site of the so-called New Castle, built in 1080 by William the Conqueror's son, Robert Curthose. It was after this edifice that the town was named. The New Castle itself was constructed on the site of the Roman Pons Aelius (Bridge of Hadrian). Admission: £1.50, 50p concessions. 0191 232 7938

BALTIC, THE CENTRE FOR CONTEMPORARY ART, Gateshead Quays. Opened in July 2002, BALTIC is the major new centre for contemporary visual art and stands grandly above the water on the south bank. Five galleries and more than 3,000 square metres. It is housed in an old grain store, part of the old Baltic Flour Mills (*see above*).
0191 478 1810| balticmill.com

THE SAGE GATESHEAD, opened 2005. Lord Foster's contribution to the Geordie quayside, a music complex catering for classical, folk, jazz, brass and choral. This is the home of the Northern Sinfonia. Ticket Office - 0191 443 4661. Switchboard - 0191 443 4666. Music Education Centre Reception - 0191 443 4627. Brasserie Bookings - 0191 443 4654. Coats Desk - 0191 443 4634.
www.thesagegateshead.org

GATESHEAD MILLENNIUM BRIDGE
Takes walkers and cyclists from Newcastle's Quayside across to Gateshead Quays and Baltic Square and the Baltic contemporary art gallery. The bridge opens and closes like a giant eyelid, allowing shipping to pass. Spectacularly lit at night, like many who inhabit these once louche purlieus.

GRAINGER TOWN - a rejuvenated architectural treasure trove with some of Britain's greatest examples of Georgian and Victorian architecture, plus many of the city's top shops.

CHINATOWN - around Stowell St. Restaurant standard is good and prices reasonable. Exotic supermarkets and craft shops.

 PUBS & FOOD

PUBS

THE CUMBERLAND ARMS, James Place St, Ouseburn, Byker, NE6 1LD. Described by James May (in the programme with Oz Clarke) as 'one of the best pubs I have ever been in.' Piece of living history and only a short hop from the Quayside. Great beer and now doing accommodation.

CROWN POSADA , The Side. 0191 232 1269 Known locally as The Coffin because it is long and narrow, this is probably the city's best pub. There's no TV, and any music comes either from an old gramophone or the mouths of revellers. There are stained-glass windows, interesting ceilings, wood-clad walls and six excellent ales. Legend has it that the pub was bought by a Spanish sea captain for his mistress.

THE CYCLE HUB is situated beside the River Tyne a few hundred metres from the Blinking Eye / Millennium Bridge (if heading eastwards) and is the perfect place to stop for lunch or a final re-fuelling before the last miles of the C2C if heading to Tynemouth. It provides bike hire for the route and has a workshop too should your bike be in need of some TLC, or just the tyres pumping up! It is also home to Saddle Skedaddle Cycling Holidays who provide lots of trip packages and support options along the route.
The Cycle Hub, Ouseburn, Newcastle, NE6 1BU
0191276 7250, enquiries@thecyclehub.org, thecylehub.org

BRIDGE HOTEL , Castle Square.0191 232 6400 Big pub looking across at the castle keep. Nestles into the side of the mighty high level bridge. Patio garden at the rear encircled by the old town wall affords great views of the river.

THE OLD GEORGE INN, Cloth Market. 0191 269 3061. One of the 'Toon's' oldest establishments, you reach it down a cobbled back alley. Despite being in the middle of the frantic Bigg Market, where every night is like New Year's Eve in other towns, it is a grownup drinking spot.

DUKE OF WELLINGTON, High Bridge. 0191 261 8852 This pub is a one-room wonder, stocking lots of fast changing ales from all over the country. Used to be run by a 50-stone landlord, one of the biggest men in the world, whose bulk would have barred him from entering the Posada.

BODEGA, 125 Westgate Road. 0191 221 1552 According to the Good Beer Guide the highlight of this pub, apart from the range of real ales, is the original twin glass ceiling domes. The pub is a hit with the city's culturati as it stands next to the Tyne Theatre and Opera House. It is a great melting pot as it is also popular with football fans.

HOTSPUR , 103 Percy Street. 0191 232 4352 Popular, single-roomed, city centre pub with four guest ales close to the shopping centre. Busy, and busier still when United are on telly.

RESTAURANTS

CHINESE

LAU'S BUFFET KING , 44-50 Stowell St. 0191 261 8868 If you want to pack in the protein for the following day's ride, this is the place. It's a hugely popular all-you-can-eat' that seats 300.

KING NEPTUNE , 34-36 Stowell St. 0191 261 6657 Award winning food. Sumptuous surroundings. You can't go too far wrong anywhere in Stowell St.

ITALIAN

MARCO POLO, 33 Dean St. 0191 232 5533 Friendly, efficient service. Traditional fare, dim lighting. Marco's is an institution.

UNO'S , 18 Sandhill, Quayside. 0191 261 5264 Offers some cheap and cheerful choices. Popular with celebrities.

MODERN

CAFE 21, 19-21 Queen St, Quayside. 0191 222 0755 Simply one of the best restaurants in the north east, you need to book well in advance.

AMER'S, 34 Osbourne Rd, Jesmond. 0191 281 5377. Top place serving good and inexpensive grub means you HAVE to book. Cosy and stylish modern cooking in a trendy spot.

THE BISCUIT FACTORY, 16 Stoddart St. 0191 260 5411. Between Quayside and Jesmond in a 1930s converted factory – the sort of place that is now as voguish as it was hitherto ghastly. Fine cooking in a Modern Art gallery.

THE CYCLE HUB
OUSEBURN, NEWCASTLE, NE6 1BU

Situated beside the River Tyne a few hundred metres from the Blinking Eye / Millennium Bridge (if heading eastwards), The Cycle Hub is the perfect place to stop for lunch or a final re-fuelling before the last miles of the C2C if heading to Tynemouth. It provides bike hire for the route and has a workshop too should your bike be in need of some TLC, or just the tyres pumping up! It is also home to Saddle Skedaddle Cycling Holidays who provide lots of trip packages / support options along the route.

0191276 7250
enquiries@thecyclehub.org
www.thecyclehub.org

ACCOMMODATION

There are plenty of hotels and guest houses. The Jesmond area, just north of the centre, is full of places to stay and lively night spots. If you're overnighting in the city, there are hotels near the waterfront, down on the fashionable Quayside. For a full list of hotels, call the Tourist Information Centre:
0191 277 8000
Newcastle Gateshead Accommodation Guide
ngi@ngi.org.uk
Newcastle Gateshead Initiative
0191 243 8800.
Many cyclists enjoy the Quayside area, close to the Central Station. The atmosphere is vibrant, but the hotels, as in most city centres, can be expensive.

The Cumberland Arms, James Place St, Ouseburn, Byker, Newcastle upon Tyne, NE6 1LD

Run by: Duty Manager

A traditional pub with four beautiful en-suite rooms, all with super kingsize beds. Ideally placed to explore the city and the quayside or you could choose to settle in and enjoy the open fires, real ale and cider, gigs, traditional sessions and great nights of spoken word and comedy. The pub offers food boards to accompany your beer: cheese, pâté and pork pies plus homemade scotch eggs, and other treats. Featured by Oz Clarke and James May on TV, it is described in Lonely Planet magazine by the former as one of the 'best pubs I've ever been in.'

Rooms: 4D/T.
B&B: D/T £80, S £70,
Family £100 (inc continental b'fast).
Opening hours: 3pm -11pm Mon, Tues, Thurs & Sun; and 3pm - 12am Wed, Fri & Sat.
Food served: non-stop.
Packed lunch: £5
Secure cycle storage.
Drying facilities. Visit England 3-star Inn.
0191 265 1725 \ 0191 265 6151
info@thecumberlandarms.co.uk
thecumberlandarms.co.uk

Tynemouth & Whitley Bay

A couple of miles down river on the opposite bank sits Jarrow, home of the Venerable Bede, and the Bede's World Museum. It was also the starting point for the Jarrow March. Two hundred strikers descended upon London in 1936 and made one of the most striking political statements in British working class history.

As you approach the Royal Quays North Sea Ferry Terminus make sure you follow the signs (easily missed) and go to the LEFT of the Wet'n'Wild water centre (you can't miss it - the giant flume tubes look like part of some space-age factory). Follow the path through landscaped public gardens in which an incongruous cluster of wooden sea groynes stand, as if awaiting tidal erosion. Turn left just beyond them, by a faded waysign - do not head back in the direction of the Amsterdam and Bergen ferry terminal - and go through the modern housing estate. To the right, pleasure craft and fishing boats should be bobbing around at their moorings.

Keep following the C2C, Route 72 and Route 10 signs (they are clustered together) and you will find yourself passing through another modern housing estate. You are now in North Shields, erstwhile home of comedian, Stan Laurel.

Following the signs, descend a steep flight of stone steps to the fish quays. You will arrive outside a former pub called the Chain Locker, opposite the ferry terminus to South Shields. The view across the Tyne on a good day is worth a pause. You can see, in the far distance, the elegant 19th century façade of the clock tower of South Shields town hall.

Cafes, stores and splendid fish & chip restaurants run the length of the North Shields Quays. This is where Danish and Polish sailors used to integrate vigorously with the local community at a den of iniquity called the Infamous Jungle, now known as the Collingwood Buildings. You soon round the point where the North Sea meets the Tyne. Welcome to Tynemouth. You pass the 11th century Priory and Castle, and the handsome statue of the man who really won the Battle of Trafalgar in 1805, Admiral Lord Collingwood. Nelson's unassuming and undersung deputy single-handedly took on five French warships

for a full hour before the rest of the English fleet caught up. He assumed command upon Nelson's death half-way through the battle, and is Tynemouth's most famous son.

This is a stylish little haven centred upon Front St, a handsome wide avenue built for eating, drinking and promenading. The village is a conservation area of architectural gems from the 18th and 19th centuries. The stretch of shore from here, through Cullercoats and up to Whitley Bay, is known as Newcastle's Côte d'Azur. You will note that there is cycle parking in Tynemouth and Whitley Bay, just over a mile up the coast.

This is where you finish, though there is no obvious place to crack a bottle of Evian Water. No matter. It is a delightful spot and there is bags of accommodation in Whitley Bay, just round the corner (plus a couple of B&Bs in Tynemouth itself).

Don't forget to dip your front wheel in the water.

🍴 WHERE TO EAT

GIORGIO'S PIZZERIA & RESTAURANT, Front St. 0191 257 3758.

GIBRALTAR ROCK East St. 0191 258 5655

THE GATE OF INDIA, 40 Front St. 0191 258 3453.

CELEBRATING THE END

There are several good pubs in Tynemouth. Here are three recommendations.

TYNEMOUTH LODGE HOTEL, Tynemouth Rd. A real locals' pub frequented by the lifeboatmen. Great beers and often very busy. It's at the top of that steep climb out of the North Shields fish quays, on the edge of Tynemouth. Worth tracking back if you have got the energy.

THE TURKS HEAD, Front St. Otherwise known as the Stuffed Dog because of Willie the Scottish collie, whose 130 year old taxidermised remains sit in a glass box looking at the bar. Willie came down from the Scottish Borders with a herd of sheep and a shepherd, but somehow got separated from them and spent the rest of his life waiting and pining in Tynemouth for his lost master. A tale of epic proportions told in detail on a plaque. Good Courage Directors, regular guest ales. Food served all day.

HUGO'S, Front Street. A handsome establishment, it is one of eight pubs in this small town. Has a changing selection of hand-pulled ales. Food served.

Whitley Bay and Tynemouth adjoin each other so are equally suitable for that final night. It is impossible not to notice that this resort, with its Pleasure Dome, Spanish City and seaside villas, is geared up for tourism and little else. Every other building offers food, drink or accommodation - or all three. Whitley Bay is a striking seaside resort, and in the past was a thriving holiday resort for tourists. It is currently attempting to rediscover its former glory, when smart Geordies would jockey for position on Newcastle Coast's promenade.

PUBS

FITZGERALDS Half-timbered Victorian pub. Good food and drink and a lively night spot.

BRIAR DENE A former tollhouse with a well-earned reputation for good quality beer and food,' according to the Good Beer Guide (CAMRA Books: £12.99). It overlooks St Mary's lighthouse and the sea. Serves good food.

ROCKCLIFFE ARMS Attractive one-roomed pub with stained-glass, & two distinct drinking areas separated by a partition. Proper ` locals' pub.

ACCOMMODATION

The Metropolitan, 13 Esplanade, Whitley Bay, NE26 2AH
Run by: Andrew Stephenson & Stephen Dodds
Sleeps up to 24 so is ideal for groups. Contemporary 4-star B&B on the quiet area of Whitley Bay, but only a couple of minutes walk from the award-winning beach and short stroll to the vibrant town centre. Highly recommended on all review sites and currently voted the the top place to stay in Tyne & Wear on Tripadvisor. Free wireless internet throughout, all rooms are en-suite and the room facilities include 32" LCD TV, iPod dock, radio alarm clock, DVD player, Freeview, complimentary hospitality tray, luxury toiletries and towels. Free on-street parking.
Rooms: 1S, 3T, 1D, 1F (sleeps up to six) plus pop-up beds.
B&B: from £35 (£30 if sharing family room).
£45 single occ.
Eve meal: no, but lots of choice nearby.
Pk lunch: by arrangement.
Secure lock up. Drying facilities.
0191 253 4941
info@themetropolitan.co
themetropolitan.co

THE REIVERS ROUTE

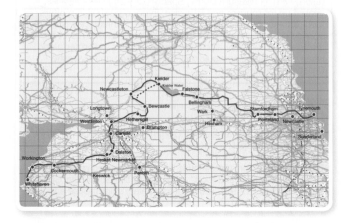

The Reivers Route opened in 1998 and is 173 miles long. It is known as the Return C2C as it takes you from the end of the C2C all the way back to its start, heading east to west. It is a great route in its own right – in some ways superior to the C2C as much of it is through real wilderness – but it has never had as much attention and money spent on it. Only recently adopted as part of the National Cycle Network, the tricky bits around Kielder have all been put right with new signage this year (2015). This is tremendous news and should lead to fewer complaints about getting lost.

Thanks here go to the cycle route management unit set up to work closely with local authorities and Sustrans. Numbers reported cycling the route have steadily been going up since the disastrous summer of 2008 and the grimly wet July and August of 2009.

As with the C2C, the gradients along Reivers work in the cyclist's favour. The route winds its way through some of the wildest and most untouched countryside in the UK. It starts at the mouth of the mighty Tyne, finishes on the Cumbrian coast and along the way riders follow the shores of Kielder Water – Europe's largest man-made lake – before crossing the Border for a brief foray into Scotland.

Emerging from the post-industrial and partially regenerated suburbs of Newcastle, the route quickly threads its way into the first gentle then rugged countryside of the Northumberland National Park.

There are fine views across the towering Cheviots before you become immersed in the forest tracks around Kielder, where some of the options are suitable only for MTBs. But as I say, the signage has been improved and there is now less chance of you ending up in the middle of nowhere on a track completely unsuited to your bike.

After the Borders you reach Carlisle before heading down through the northern Lakes, through some quiet but stunning sections which somehow escape the notice of the masses. Enjoy the ride from Kielder to Newcastleton and make sure to spend a night at this far-flung agricultural village, with its two excellent pub/hotels.

This is truly isolated terrain. You could be in the wilderness of Sutherland or Ross-shire when suddenly you stumble across such gems as Hesket Newmarket, with its own excellent micro-brewery before heading through some of the most untouched and beautiful stretches of the Lake District, taking you down to Cockermouth and Bassenthwaite. There is much satisfaction to be had from making these discoveries.

MAPS

Though I provide some mapping in this book, and there is now good waymarking along the way, you would be advised to get the official route map from the website c2c-guide.co.uk.

If you don't mind bulk and cost, the new OS Landranger maps have full route details, though the older ones may not have Route 10 marked.

OS Landranger maps: (1:50,000) 88, 87, 80, 79, 86, 85, 90 & 89 (in east to west sequence).

Stirling Surveys:
01786 479866
stirlingsurveys.co.uk/footprint

Sustrans:
0117 929 0888

Cordee Books & Maps:
01455 611185
cordee.co.uk

GETTING THERE

The Reivers trail starts at Tynemouth Harbour, a scenic spot looking out to the North Sea with the Priory and Castle the first thing you see when you turn your face inland.

To get there, first head for Newcastle. Then you have the choice of riding out to the starting point along the north bank of the Tyne, taking a taxi or taking your car.

Aim for Tynemouth station, and when you get there, turn left into Station Terrace and first right into Huntingdon Place. Straight ahead until you join Front Street, which takes you to the coast. Turn right onto Pier Road and head for the car park. Then let the fun begin.

RAIL

Travel details are also included at the start of the C2C guide: Pages 18 - 21

There are direct train services from most cities in Britain to Newcastle Central Station.

Newcastle is served by National Express, Virgin Cross Country and Regional Railways. It takes 2 hours 45 minutes from London, and 1 hour 20 minutes from Edinburgh.
0191 221 3156
(station direct line).

To book train seats:

National Rail Enquiry Service
08457 484950

Virgin (west coast)
08457 222333

East Coast
08457 225225

ROAD

Newcastle is easily accessible by car from all parts of the UK. The A1(M) goes through the middle of it. If you are coming by car, there is limited secure parking in the city centre, near Central Station, for a horrible £15 a day.
0191 243 8294

WAYMARK

The route is now waymarked with a red NCN direction sign complete with the word REIVERS and the route number. These are posted at junctions and other strategic spots. Occasionally the road surface is signed; sometimes there are just little plastic stickers stuck to gates and lamp-posts. Signage is not always brilliant, but with sharp eyes and the use of a map you should not get lost. Having said that, sections at the beginning and end have much improved since it became part of the NCN, despite the trashing and snaffling meted out by vandals and souvenir hunters.

REIVERS HISTORY
Tales of blood and guts

As you will probably know, the word Reiver means plunderer. The route is named after the murdering bandits who ran a medieval equivalent of Cosa Nostra.

This was the Chicago or Sicily of its time, when marauding clans terrorised both the English and Scottish sides of the Border for 350 years, right up to the 17th century. They lived by cattle rustling, kidnapping, extortion, arson and murder. The route passes many castles like Bew Castle as well as a number of fortified farmhouses like Askerton Castle, all of which reveal the defensive needs of the area as well as its rich heritage.

Despite the cosy thematising that has been perpetrated by tourism to give the past a false appeal, there is nothing remotely quaint or faintly honourable about Reiving; many of the families were happy to swing both ways, fighting for the English if the price was right, or vice versa.

One family, the Grahams, were so infamous that their surnames were banned by law, so the Grahams changed them to Maharg (Graham backwards), which later also became McHarg.

Indeed, the word 'blackmail' comes from the Reivers: a farmer paid 'blackmail' – rent in the form of cattle instead of the legal 'whitemail', which was paid in silver, to a powerful Reiver who would give him 'protection' in return.

Roll call of guilty names...

Archbold; Armstrong; Beattie; Bell; Burns; Carleton; Carlisle; Carnaby; Carrs; Carruthers; Chamberlain; Charlton; Collingwood; Crichtons; Crisp; Croziers; Cuthbert; Dacre; Davidson; Dixon; Dodd; Douglas; Dunne; Elliot; Fenwick; Forster; Graham; Gray; Hall; Hedley; Henderson; Heron; Hetherington; Hume; Irvine; Irving; Johnston; Kerr; Laidlaw; Little; Lowther; Maxwell; Milburn; Musgrove; Nixon; Noble; Ogle; Oliver; Potts; Pringle; Radcliffe; Reade; Ridley; Robson; Routledge; Rutherford; Salkeld; Scott; Selby; Shaftoe; Storey; Simpson; Tait; Taylor; Trotter; Turnbull; Wake; Watson; Wilson; Woodrington; Young.

18 miles (11 miles traffic-free)

TYNEMOUTH & WHITLEY BAY

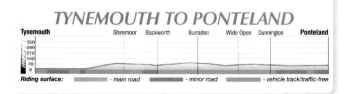

TYNEMOUTH TO PONTELAND

Tynemouth | Shiremoor | Backworth | Burradon | Wide Open | Dunnington | Ponteland

350 · 280 · 210 · 140 · 70 · 0

Riding surface: ▨ - main road ▨ - minor road ▨ - vehicle track/traffic-free

ABOUT THE TOWN

Those of you doing the round trip will recognise the first three miles of the route, since it is the same as the last three miles of the C2C, but at North Shields it executes a smart right turn and off you go towards the Scottish Border.

There is plenty to do in Tynemouth, which has monuments testifying to a history ranging from Roman times (it is the start of the Hadrian's Cycleway) to the area's recent industrial heritage. Wallsend, nearby, is ideal for the Hadrian's Wall experience. The fort at Segedunum was brought back to life at a cost of £9 million, with the only restored Roman bathhouse in Britain.

In medieval times, it was the preferred residence of the queens of both Edward I and Edward II, while their husbands were off fighting the Scots – successfully in the case of the first, less so for his son.

Down river, on the opposite bank, sits Jarrow, home of the Venerable Bede, and the Bede's World Museum. It was also the starting point for the Jarrow March, when 200 protesters descended upon London in 1936 and made one of the most striking political statements in working class history.

❋ For all ACCOMMODATION, PUBS AND EATERY details for Tynemouth and Whitley Bay: see pages 193 - 196 →

▶ DIRECTIONS

The Stirling map has three large-scale sections showing the best route out of Tynemouth, which I reproduce with their kind permission. There is an alternative route out via Whitley Bay, but the main recommendation is as follows.

1 Start from the car park off Pier Road, facing the Castle and Priory, and take the path along the estuary. Turn left into Cliffords Fort and immediately right into Union Road, then left through the fish quays of North Shields. There may not be so many fishing boats now, but there are many quality fish and chip shops. Union Quay becomes Bell Street, Liddle Street and finally Clive Street.

2 Go right at the end of Clive St, then first left into Addison St, which soon becomes Lawson St. At the T-junction with Dock Rd, head left following the cycle path around the marina. The path takes you in a loop under the road and at the far end of the marina go right, passing to the right of Wet 'n Wild, taking you under the A187 and shortly onto the old rail line, via St John's Green.

3 Follow the path to the right, along the cycle path parallel with Coble Dene, opposite the huge shopping centre at Royal Quays. This is where the Fjordline and DFDS ferries come in. You now cross Howdon Rd (A187). This brings you to St John's Green. Turn right past Percy Main Station. You will shortly be on the Waggonways, a disused railway line which passes the Stephenson Railway Museum. The famous family hailed from near Wylam, west of Newcastle on the Tyne and the museum has some original locomotives (0191 200 7145)

PONTELAND → BELLINGHAM

33 miles (3 miles traffic-free)

STAMFORDHAM

▶ DIRECTIONS

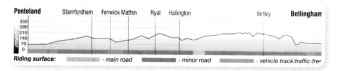

| Ponteland | Stamfordham | Fenwick Matfen | Ryal | Hallington | | Birtley | **Bellingham** |

Riding surface: — main road — minor road — vehicle track/traffic-free

Out of the urban sprawl and into the countryside

Stamfordham is a handsome and planned estate village with a large green, a pond and a couple of pubs, the Bay Horse and the Swinburne Arms. The church may be Victorian, but most of the village is stone-built and 18th century. The name Stamfordham is Old English for `homestead by the stony ford'. It was once part-owned by Balliol College, Oxford.

- Once out of Tynemouth and past Shiremoor, you are clear of the urban sprawl and can settle down to enjoy the countryside.

- Go left over the level crossing and through Backworth, Burradon and Seaton Burn, taking you past the Big Waters Nature Reserve, Dinnington and up to prosperous Ponteland, where most of the Newcastle United stars live.

- After crossing the golf course you arrive in the village at the Diamond Inn. There is a coffee shop to the left and you can lunch at the pub or the Smithy Bistro (also immediately on your left). But in reality, having covered only 16 miles or so, you are unlikely to require much or want to stop for long. If you do take a break, then there are lots of shops, plus pubs and restaurants to be found here.

- Once past Ponteland, you are away from urban life for most of the trip. Go straight across the crossroads but look out for a sign to the right, where you double back on yourself before taking a left hairpin through the smart housing estate of Darras Hall. At the T-junction at the end of the estate go right, then left towards Donkins House Farm before taking a track up to the right. This will take you via the back lanes to the lovely village of Stamfordham.

163

ACCOMMODATION

Church House, Stamfordham, Northumberland NE18 0PB
Run by: Mrs Viv Fitzpatrick

17th century house of great character on south side of a pretty village green. Private residence, good breakfast, welcoming hosts. Church House looks directly onto the common land. Safe storage for cycles. Soup and sandwiches available at the Swinburne pub and David will take you and pick you up from Matfen Golf Club if you fancy something more substantial. Many cyclists stop in Ponteland for supper before arriving.

Rooms: 3T.
B&B: £32.50-£45.
Pk lunch: £5.
On route.
Pub: adjacent.
01661 886736
bedandbreakfast@stamfordham.fsbusiness.co.uk

Matfen Hall, Matfen, Northumberland NE20 0RH
Run by: Duty Manager

Set in 300 acres of sculpted parkland, this great ancestral home of Sir Hugh Blackett was converted into a luxury spa and golf hotel in 1999. It is one of the great hotels of the North East and is an ideal spot for groups seeking (affordable) comfort in the eastern sector of the route. The Library restaurant has 2 AA Rosettes and if you have the time and energy, there's a 27-hole golf course.

B&B: from £37.50 (from £75 per room).
Rooms: 53.
Eve meal: three restaurants to choose from. Snacks and sandwiches in the Keeper's Lodge. 3-course approx £21 in Conservatory and around £40 for 3-courses in the fine dining Library Restaurant.
Pk lunch: please pre-order. Secure cycle storage. Drying facilities.
01661 886500
info@matfenhall.com
matfenhall.com

DIRECTIONS

- Don't miss the sign for the route out of the village! In two miles you will pass through the tiny hamlet of Fenwick and a couple of miles beyond that is Matfen. A great new overnight stop is the highly luxurious (but affordable) Matfen Hall.

BELLINGHAM

ABOUT THE VILLAGE

Where Scots and robbers met their match in stone and blood

This ancient little market town, pronounced 'Bellinjum', nestles at the foot of some of the wildest and most barren fells in Northumberland. There are medieval references to Bellingham Castle belonging to the King of Scotland's forester, but sadly no trace remains.

St Cuthbert's Church is unusual with its stone roof and extremely narrow windows. Both features were included as a defence against the marauding Scots who twice burnt it to the ground. In its graveyard lies the famous 'Lang Pack' grave which is associated with one of Northumberland's most notorious tales of murder, intrigue and deception. One day a pedlar (a tinker, not a cyclist) came to Lee Hall, the home of a landed local gentleman and asked if he could leave his backpack there while he attended to an errand in the village. The maid said yes, and it was left in the kitchen.

She noted how big and broad the conical shaped pack was, but thought no more about it. The gypsy failed to return that day and during the night she came down with a candle and noticed the pack had marginally moved. She ran and fetched old Richards, the wrinkled retainer, who blasted it with a blunderbuss. There followed much blood and whimpering, then silence. Inside was the corpse of a criminal whose dastardly plan was to rob and murder the household in the dead of night. He got more than he bargained for. His grave lies in the churchyard, dated 1723. A plot well foiled!

There is also St Cuthbert's Well, dedicated to the saint and a welcome addition for thirsty Pennine Way walkers, as it is right next to the pathway for Britain's most famous walk. On the edge of the Northumberland National Park on the North Tyne river, the Bellingham area is well known for its fishing, as it is a major spawning ground for salmon, sea trout and brown trout. It has two caravan sites, a campsite, four pubs and hotels and just about everything else including a haberdashery, gym and library. The annual agricultural show in the summer (on the last Saturday in August) is a big attraction with a country fair and Cumberland/Westmorland wrestling, all done to the skirl of the magnificent Northumbrian pipes.

▶ DIRECTIONS

The route now goes out of Bellingham following signs for Wark and Hexham. Cross the North Tyne, turn right across Shitlington Common and follow the south bank. You are now in the Northumberland National Park. Continue for about 4 miles to the T-junction where you go right back over the Tyne. There's a climb up to Lanehead then a left. You are on the Falstone road.

PLACES OF INTEREST

Hareshaw Linn superb waterfall, a half-mile walk.

St Cuthbert's (Cuddy's) Well Reputed to be healing water.

Tourist Information Centre Main St 01434 220616

Heritage Centre. Local history. 01434 220050. Excellent background about Reivers, Border counties railway which ran from Hexham to Bellingham and across the border. Recreation of old mine workings, plus shop of local early 20-c photographer W.P. Collier.

 ## BIKE REPAIRS:

Village Country Store
01434 220027

ACCOMMODATION

Riverdale Hall Hotel, Bellingham, Northumberland NE48 2JT
Run by: Duty Manager
Set on the banks of the North Tyne river at the gateway to Northumberland National Park. Riverdale Hall Hotel is a Victorian country house hotel boasting its own indoor heated swimming pool and sauna, cosy bar and lounge with open log fires. Riverdale serves bar meals, real ales and much more. There's an award winning restaurant and a beer garden with stunning views. Private Fishing beats and fantastic moorland golf course nearby set this hotel apart from all the rest. Riverdale offers secure storage for bikes and discounted rates for cycling parties, with free use of our pool and sauna to help relax those muscles!
B&B: from £35.
01434 220254
reservations@riverdalehallhotel.co.uk
riverdalehallhotel.co.uk

Riverdale Hall Hotel
COUNTRY HOUSE & RESTAURANT

Award Winning Restaurant, Indoor Pool, Sauna, Cricket Field & Salmon River in its own delightful grounds

01434 220254
reservations@riverdalehallhotel.co.uk

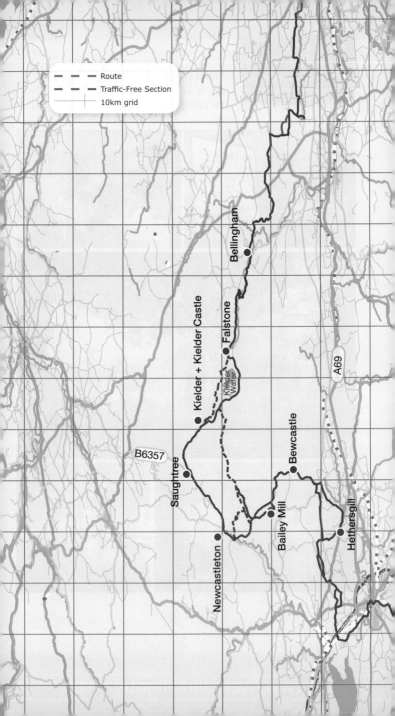

Route
Traffic-Free Section
10km grid

Bellingham

Kielder + Kielder Castle
Falstone

Kielder Water

B6357

Saughtree

Bewcastle

Bailey Mill

A69

Newcastleton

Hethersgill

BELLINGHAM → KIELDER

22 miles (4 miles traffic-free)

FALSTONE

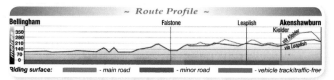

~ Route Profile ~

Bellingham   Falstone   Leaplish   Akenshawburn
Kielder
via Kielder
via Leaplish

Riding surface: ▬▬▬ - main road ▬▬▬ - minor road ▬▬▬ - vehicle track/traffic-free

▶ DIRECTIONS

To find the route out of Bellingham follow the signs for Wark and Hexham. Cross the North Tyne, turn right and follow the south bank. You are now in the Northumberland National Park. Continue for about 4 miles to the T-junction where you go right back over the Tyne. There follows a climb into Lanehead followed by a left. Close beyond the remains of Tarset Castle you turn onto the Falstone road.

The secluded hamlet of Falstone lost nearly 80% of its parish under the waters of Kielder Reservoir. Today the village is a tranquil beauty spot surrounded by trees, and is a good stopping place, with post office, shop and pub.

A tributary to the Tyne bubbles its way through the centre of the village and, depending on the time of year, it is possible to see dippers, heron, cormorants, goosanders, and with luck you may witness the miraculous sight of salmon spawning.

ABOUT THE VILLAGE

From the 1st century AD the Northumbrian uplands fell under the control of an expanding Roman Empire. The principal bases of Roman power in the area lay at the forts of Risingham (Habitancum) and High Rochester (Bremenium), both on Dere Street, the main road into Scotland, and to the west at Bewcastle (Fanum Cocidii). Falstone is first recorded in the form 'Foustan' in 1317. This is thought to refer to the 'speckled stone' of the distinctive rocky outcrop, which acquired a religious significance in Medieval times.

New Lakeside Way transforms Kielder

The Kielder section recently benefited from £3 million worth of tracks around both the north and south shores of the mighty lake. There are consequently 25.5 miles (plus the dam) of the finest track. At £43 a metre, this 'compact dust' path is between 2 and 2.5 metres wide. Both shores are now equally accessible, though the north is longer and even more scenic. It is a multi-user track so watch out for horse riders and walkers, though the majority of exploiting this new resource are cyclists. (The dreaded 5C section has been ploughed into oblivion, I am delighted to report).

North or south? Your call...

- SOUTH: If you wish to take the southern shore then turn left and head over the dam after Falstone. This will take you past the Tower Knowe Visitor Centre and Leaplish Waterside Park.

  2.5 miles after Leaplish, the path bears left under the road bridge arriving at the Lewisburn suspension bridge, winner of a national Better Buildings' Award. The path around Leiwisburn Inlet makes for a rewarding detour, however if you are intent on making your way to the Border, as you reach the bridge, exit to your left to join the forestry road which leads along the burn to The Forks and Akenshawburn.

  If you wish to go to Newcastleton (excellent overnight facilities) then you can either a) go right for Kielder then take the Saughtree road (the softer option); or b) go straight on for six or so roller coaster miles and head for Newcastleton just beyond Kershope (a very winding and steep route) or carry on to Kershope Bridge and take the Sorbietrees road.

- NORTH: This used to be a tough option. Now it's a doddle! The northern route takes you past Kielder Castle and its visitor centre. It is an exciting and scenic area with a number of viewpoints, artworks and points of interest. Watch out for the suspension bridge at the western end. From Kielder Castle you can either take the Saughtree road to Newcastleton or make your way back down the south shore to Lewisburn Inlet where, after crossing the bridge, turn right and follow the forest track along the burn en route to Scotland.

  There are facilities at Kielder plus limited accommodation. You will briefly join the Newcastleton road before skirting off towards Akenshawburn, unless you are heading for an overnight in this fine Borders stronghold, in which case go right onto the main road at Kielder and up through Saughtree and thence Newcastleton.

- Newcastleton is the only beacon of civilisation (apart from accommodation around Bailey Mill) between Kielder and the village of Hethersgill, some 20 miles away.

ACCOMMODATION

The Pheasant Inn, Stannersburn, Falstone, by Kielder Water, NE48 1DD
Run by: Robin Kershaw
Traditional and unspoilt country inn ideal for groups. The Pheasant has featured in Alistair Sawday's Special Places to Stay and the Good Pub Guide for the past 20 years or so. The food is renowned as is the beer: game pies, salmon and local lamb, as well as wonderful Northumbrian cheeses. Recently refurbished and awarded TripAdvisor's Certificate of Excellence for 2014, and yet another VisitBritain award for its breakfasts and the 2015 AA Dinner Award. Robin has been running the place since 1986 and is a seasoned Reivers' host.
Rooms: 4D, 3T, 1F (sleeps 4).
B&B: £45-£50.
Eve meal: from £17 for 3-courses.
Pk lunch: please pre-order.
Secure lock up. On route.
01434 240382
stay@thepheasantinn.com
thepheasantinn.com

KIELDER

ABOUT THE VILLAGE

At the head of the reservoir, Kielder was once a wild and uncultivated fastness, surrounded by moors and bogs. It is now a purpose-built forestry village cocooned by alpine spruce and pine trees. Before the turn of the century Kielder Castle, which stands guard over the village, would have been hidden and alone at the valley head. It was built in 1775 by the Duke of Northumberland as his hunting lodge. Shooting parties travelled from London on the sleeper and were met at the station by pony and trap. To carry home a bag of 200 brace of grouse and blackcock in a day was not unusual. The village is a small oasis for the cyclist, with a shop, pub and post office. The whole area is now far more accessible as multi-purpose tracks have been put in from the dam almost as far as the village, thanks to the Kielder Partnership. This avoids roads which, during the summer, become horribly busy.

 ## PLACES OF INTEREST

Kielder Castle Forest Shop, tea room, WCs
Kielder Castle Visitor Centre 01434 250 209

WHERE TO EAT

THE ANGLERS ARMS 01434 250 072

Kielder Water

A wild and romantic place, Kielder Water is in the heart of Border Reiver country. It is hard to imagine the cattle rustling, kidnapping and arson that flourished here in the 15th and 16th centuries. Today Kielder's stunning scenery, peace and quiet welcome all visitors. There is a wealth of facilities for the cyclist here. Northumbria Water, who created the reservoir, has been responsible for a good deal of the inspiration behind the Reivers Cycle Route.

🔭 PLACES OF INTEREST

Tower Knowe Visitor Centre: 0870 2403549. An Information Centre with extensive gift shop and audio visual exhibition. Situated on the south bank very near the dam wall. Open daily 10-4/5. There is a ferry point, souvenir and fishing shop, exhibition centre, picnic area, extensive lavatory facilities, self-guided trails, a sailing club and a restaurant.

Leaplish Waterside Park: 0870 240 3549. Heated swimming pool and sauna, campsite, accommodation together with a licensed restaurant, sculpture trail, bird of prey centre, and much more. Open from April-October.

Kielder Ferry Service: 0870 240 3549. 80-seater cruiser takes you round lake, from Tower Knowe to Leaplish to Kielder Castle. Facilities on board include bar, commentary, shop, heated lounge and toilets.

Kielder Water Club: sailing club and yacht club plus a water-ski club. Watercraft hire: 01434 250217. Range of canoes, kayaks, toppers, wayfarers and dinghies.

Cycling: yes, even cycling. Aside from the Reivers, there are many different routes around Kielder which might interest those of you who are doing a detour here, or perhaps meeting up with the family. Get a 'Cycling at Kielder' brochure from Tower Knowe or Leaplish Waterside Park.

Kielder Castle: 01434 250209. Former hunting lodge of the Duke of Northumberland overlooks Kielder Village and is open daily from April to October.

ACCOMMODATION

Twenty Seven B&B
Run by: Jill & Terry Gregg
Cosy former forester's cottage, with a family room which can be let out as single, twin or double plus two other rooms. Delicious breakfast at this relaxing bolt-hole in England's most remote village. Multi-fuel stoves for those chilly nights. 4-stars.
Rooms: 1D/T; 2T.
B&B: £32.
Eve meal: pse pre-order £7-£12.
Pk lunch: £5.
Free wifi. Cycle lock-up.
Laundry room.
facebook.com/TwentySevenBBKielder.
01434 250462
staykielder@gmail.com
StayKielder.co.uk

BIKE SHOPS

The Bike Place. Operates rescue service and repairs, accessories and clothing. Hire service. Big business in a small place. Unit 3, River Mead, Kielder NE48 1HX.
Ian Bell 01434 250 457

Route

Traffic-Free Section

10km grid

Kielder

Newcastleton

B6357

Bailey Mill

Bewcastle

Kirklinton

Roweltown

Westlinton

A6071

A69

A7

A689

Hethersgill

A69

Carlisle

M6

AKENSHAWBURN → KIRKLINTON

32 miles (8 miles traffic-free)

NEWCASTLETON

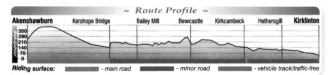

~ *Route Profile* ~

Akenshawburn Kershope Bridge Bailey Mill Bewcastle Kirkcambeck Hethersgill **Kirklinton**

Riding surface: ▬ - main road ▬ - minor road ▬ - vehicle track/traffic-free

ABOUT THE VILLAGE

Newcastleton, with its broad Georgian streets and open squares, was designed and built from scratch by the Duke of Buccleuch in 1792. Due to the changes in agriculture there was a need for more village-based employment such as handloom weaving. The houses were built with large windows to let in light for the new cottage industries. It is known locally as Copshaw Holm.

The town has a post office, several pubs, an antique shop, a bank, a grocery and several guest houses. The garage will help with bike repairs and there is also the interesting Liddesdale Heritage Centre. If your time and energy allow, don't miss a short detour to Hermitage Castle. This mysterious and magical place not only witnessed long years of turbulent border reiving, but it played host to the tragic Mary Queen of Scots when she snatched two hours' rendezvous with her lover Bothwell.

🛏 ACCOMMODATION

The Grapes Hotel, 16 Douglas Square, Newcastleton, Roxburghshire, TD9 0QD

Run by: Peter & Gail Atkinson

Family run hotel with four bars, excellent bar meals and an 'A La Carte' restaurant. Lock-up for bikes and drying facilities. In a lovely spot; lively or restful - it's up to you. The kitchens open at 11am and food is served until 9pm. A real home from home for cyclists.

Rooms: 1S, 2D, 1T, 1D/F, 1X4S, 1 bunkroom.
B&B: from £27.50 for bunkhouse. £35 D/T.
Pk lunch: made to order.
Meals: mains from £6.95.
013873 75245
info@thegrapeshotel.co.uk
thegrapeshotel.co.uk

Liddesdale Hotel, 17 Douglas Sq, Newcastleton, TD9 0QD

Run by: Tomasz Milkowski

Ideal stop-off for groups of cyclists in the central square of the village, the Liddesdale has a really good restaurant serving local produce, and a lively bar. The rooms are comfortable, en-suite, have Sky and BT Sport and there is a secure lock-up plus drying facilities. The bar is open all day and food is served from 12-2 and 5-9, so even if you're just passing through you can stop for a bite or a drink. Open fires and a warm atmosphere, the place has stepped up a gear since talented chef Tomasz recently took over in 2013.

Rooms: 1S, 2D,2T/F, 1 suite. All en-suite.

B&B: from £35 (£55 D,B&B). £45 single occ.

Pk lunch: made to order.

Meals: new Hermitage dining
restaurant £5-£18. Open 12-2; 5-8.30.
On route. AA 4-star Inn.
Discounts available for group bookings
just ring to find out more.
013873 75255
reception@theliddesdalehotel.co.uk
theliddesdalehotel.co.uk

Sorbietrees, Newcastleton , Roxburghshire, TD9 0TL

Run by: Sandy Reynolds

A warm welcome awaits you at this lovely farmhouse in spectacular countryside with AGA cooked breakfasts and a lift to the local village and back for an evening meal. Flexible accommodation for singles, couples or groups and a guest lounge with log burner where you can relax after a hard day in the saddle, or enjoy the patio and garden in warmer weather. Booking direct with Sorbietrees either on-line via the website or by telephone or email will ensure you get the best deal available

Rooms: 2D, 2T/F.

B&B: £27-£40.

Pk lunch: £4.50

Eve meal: lift to village pub.

On route.
Drying facilties. Secure lock up. Bike wash.
VisitScotland 3-star
Walkers and Cyclists Welcome award.
013873 75215
sandy.sorbietrees@btinternet.com
sorbietrees.co.uk

Newcastleton High Street

Woodside, North Hermitage St, Newcastleton,
Roxburghshire, TD9 0RZ
Run by: Michael & Marion Bogg
Charming red sandstone house built circa 1870 retains many
original Victorian features. All rooms are centrally heated and double
glazed. Large garden and parking for a dozen cars. En-suite rooms
and secure lock-up and washing facilities. 1.5 miles from 7-Stanes
mountain bike route (www.7stanes.gov.uk).
Rooms: 1S, 1D, 1T plus self-catering bungalow for six.
B&B: £27-£30.
Pk lunch: £5.
2 pubs near doorstep. On route.
Cycle storage & wash down facilities.
Free wifi.
013873 75431
mandmbogg@sky.com
woodside.newcastleton.net

BEWCASTLE

BAILEY MILL

At the southern end of Newcastleton take a left, heading up the
hill past Sorbietrees and down to Kershope Bridge, right up the
steep hill to the telephone box and onward to Bailey Mill.
Keep your eyes peeled and follow the Route 10 signs towards
Bewcastle. You will soon see a handsome cluster of white
buildings that look as if they have been transported from SW
France and carefully placed in this harsher clime. This is Bailey
Mill, an excellent stop off, whether for food and drink or an
overnight stay.

 ## ACCOMMODATION

Bailey Mill, Bailey, nr Newcastleton, Roxburghshire, TD9 0TR
Run by: Pam Copeland
Facilities for campers now include two indoor showers, while there
is room for 10 B&B guests in this charming old complex of farm
buildings. There is a hot tub and a public bar, plus restaurant. A
great stopping off point in one of the more remote areas of the
Borderlands. Secure storage, a hose to wash bikes down, plus drying
rooms. A beautiful, isolated spot where all you could need is at hand.
Rooms: Apartment with king size bed + 1S. 1 quad, 1 triple.
B&B: £28-£38.
Pk lunch: from £5.
Eve meal: from £12-£15 (3 courses).
On route.
016977 48617
info@bailey-mill.co.uk
baileymillholidays.co.uk

BEWCASTLE CROSS

The famous Bewcastle Cross (left) has survived 1300 years of relentless border weather in St Cuthbert's churchyard. The church and remains of the castle stand remote and almost alone save for a farmhouse in this forgotten outpost in a great sweep of wild and rugged countryside.

There is a display of interpretative panels nearby in the small Past & Present Heritage Centre. They tell the story of the Anglo-Saxon cross. The runic inscriptions and carving are of a very high quality for this period in history.

HETHERSGILL

ABOUT HETHERSGILL

There is not a huge amount at Hethersgill, a place whose economy has been traditionally fuelled by peat extraction. You can stop for a pint at the Black Lion pub, which belongs to the same folk who run the Drove Inn at Stapleton, near Hethersgill.

Route: From Hethersgill follow signs to Boltonfellend and head lett to Kirklinton. Here you are on the river Lyne, not far from Longtown. There are lots of tiny communities dotted around here.

▶ DIRECTIONS

- The stretch to Kircambeck is fairly straightforward. After that continue to Hethersgill by heading right at Askerton Castle, then left onto the B6318 and first right at Knorren Lodge.

- There are various accommodation choices at places such as Walton and Stapleton – none of them exactly on the route, but all worth a stopover to get a real flavour of the area.
  Two possibilities are Low Luckens and New Pallyards. To reach either, take the route past Hethersgill up to Boltonfellend. Instead of turning left on the signposted route, head straight on, bearing left at the junction with the main road. Continue across the river, taking the second left for New Pallyards, or first right

for Low Luckens. If opting for the latter, take a further right after 500m, opposite a farm a kilometre or so up the road; follow a metalled road up to Low Luckens. This delightful backwater is called Roweltown.

'Summer is for grazing, but autumn is for raiding'
The Reivers were far too busy tending crops and fattening the cattle in summer to be doing any plundering, but as soon as the crops were gathered and the horses fit they would be hot foot across the border to get down to the serious winter business of stealing each other's wives, cattle, sheep & carefully-stored winter goods again.

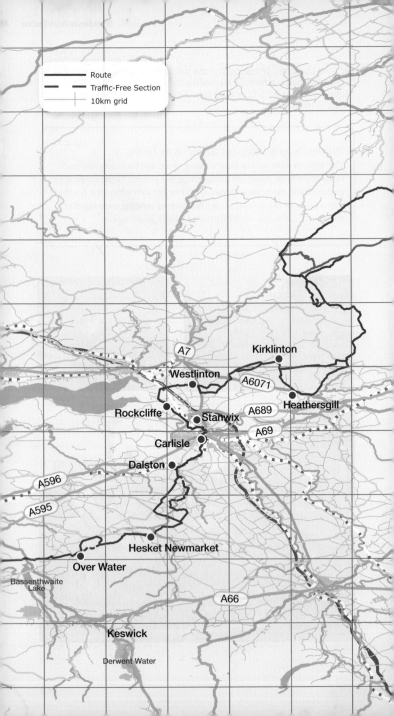

KIRKLINTON → HESKET NEWMARKET

38 miles (5 miles traffic-free)

KIRKLINTON/LONGTOWN

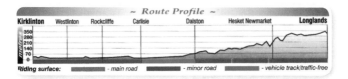

~ Route Profile ~

Kirklinton | Westlinton | Rockcliffe | Carlisle | Dalston | Hesket Newmarket | Longlands

Riding surface: ▬▬▬ - main road ▬▬▬ - minor road ▬▬▬ - vehicle track/traffic-free

ABOUT THE VILLAGE

Reiving centre that found respectability

This area which looks so cultivated and prosperous (putting aside for one minute the wretched chapter of foot and mouth disease in 2001) was once so violent that there was no proper settlement outside Carlisle until 300 years ago; that handsome bastion on Longtown's high street, the Graham Hotel, bears the name of the family who settled the town. They were also amongst the most infamous of reiving families (see p.159), whose very surname was at one stage declared illegal. That is the reason there are some 90 pele towers scattered around this area - the only way of staying alive and keeping your few head of cattle was to put them behind lock, gate and thick stone wall when the riders were abroad.

With respectability came not only the Graham Hotel, but high street banks, so if you are running low there are a couple of cash points there. The quickest way to Longtown is to turn right and head up the A6071 for two miles just beyond Kirklinton, or cross the A7 and turn right just past the Lynebank House Hotel. This takes you onto the Route 7 cycle way, the Lochs & Glens route which connects Carlisle with Glasgow.

ACCOMMODATION

Lynebank Guest House, Westlinton, nr Carlisle
Cumbria CA6 6AA
Run by: Dean Williams
Great value food and bang on the route at the junction with
the A7, this 17th century coaching house was renovated to
an 11 bedroom hotel, restaurant and bar. All rooms are en-
suite. Licensed. Secure cycle parking in landscaped courtyard.
Favourable reports from cyclists about the quality of reception
and food. Scores highly on laterooms.com. One of the most
popular stop-offs on the Reivers.
Rooms: 3S, 5D, 2T, 1F.
B&B: £32.50 - £45 (for the 4-poster).
Single occ from £40.
Pk lunch: no.
Eve meal: £10 to £20.
On route. VisitBritain 4 stars.
01228 792820
info@lynebank.com
lynebank.com

CARLISLE

✱ Full details in the Hadrian's section: Pages 221-224 →

▶ **DIRECTIONS**

●The route from Westlinton to the city takes
you down to the edge of the Solway Firth,
where the rivers Eden and Esk meet and
swell a progress across vast acres of mud
and sand until debouching into the Irish
Sea beyond Bowness and Annan. Here you
pass such erstwhile centres of shipbuilding
as Rockcliffe and other vestiges of a
prosperous past, before cutting through
a large and unattractive industrial estate.
Soon, however, you are in the heart of a
vibrant, welcoming city.

These days this great border city greets its
guests with open arms, but not so many
years ago any visitor would have been
treated with suspicion. It was the nerve-
centre for bitter feuds and bloody battles
created by the long-running dispute over

the border betwen England and Scotland. Early in its history it was an important Roman headquarters for Hadrian's Wall. In 1092 William the Conqueror's son William Rufus started to build the castle where later the unfortunate Mary Queen of Scots was incarcerated.

During a period of Scots occupation its ruler was one Macbeth; as 'Carluel' it was, according to legend, the domain of King Arthur, and the Emperor Hadrian was perhaps the first to realise that whoever held Carlisle could influence the destinies of both England and Scotland.

ACCOMMODATION

> ✱ Full details in the Hadrian's section: Pages 222-224 ➜

Crown & Mitre Hotel, English Street, Carlisle, Cumbria CA3 8HZ
01228 525491

....

Hazeldean Guest House, Orton Grange, Wigton Road, Carlisle, Cumbrian CA5 6JB
01228 711953

....

Langleigh Guest House, 6 Howard Place, Carlisle, CA1 1HR
01228 409706 / 07970 209760

....

Old Brewery Residences, Bridge Lane, Caldewgate, Carlisle CA2 5SR
01228 597352

▶ DIRECTIONS

● It is 15 miles to Hesket Newmarket. Follow the signs and keep your eyes open! I had to make a couple of attempts to get this right. Castle Way (castle on the right) then cross Bridge St, the rail line and Viaduct Estate Rd and you are, with luck, on the cycle path that takes you out towards Dalston, following the winding course of the River Caldew. At Dalston the route rejoins the road, taking you along some fairly undulating stretches until you reach the junction of the B5305 at Sour Nook, where you head left and first right up to Hesket Newmarket.

HESKET NEWMARKET

ABOUT THE VILLAGE

Ask a local the name of an ash tree and he will tell you it is a 'hesh'. Hesket means the place of the ash tree. It is a pleasant village that invites travellers to rest, featuring a medieval stone stall that was used until the late 1900s to tether bulls for the local cattle market. There is a well-stocked village shop, a post office, a couple of guest houses and the Old Crown Inn with its increasingly well-known microbrewery.

You are in the Eastern Fells of the Lake District National Park, an untouched corner of England that proved a magnet for St Mungo in the 6th century, when he came, saw and converted. Many local churches are dedicated to him, usually under his real name: Kentigern (Mungo is a nickname meaning 'dear friend'). You are about to tackle the toughest bit of the ride with some challenging up-and-down and majestic views. To the south west you will see the Lake District opening up, with great views of Skiddaw and the Uldale Fells.

ACCOMMODATION

Greenhill Farm, Hesket Newmarket, CA 7 8JG.
Run by: Arthur & Joan Todhunter
Splendid little campsite just 250m from the brewery
and pub/restaurant. Greenhill is a working farm on
the edge of this unspoilt village.
016974 78453

Denton House, Hesket Newmarket, nr Caldbeck, CA7 8JG
Run by: Susan & Alan Armstrong
Friendly atmosphere with home cooking and log fires awaits everyone
in a large 17th century house modernised to 21st century comforts.
Comfortable en-suite rooms with tea/coffee making facilities. Safe
lock up for bikes.
Rooms: 2D, 2T, 3F.
B&B: £39-£42. (single occ. supp of £6)
Pk lunch: £6.
On route. Pub nearby (with own brewery).
VisitBritain: 4 stars.
Lock-up & drying facilities.
016974 78415
dentonhnm@aol.com
dentonhouseguesthouse.co.uk

CALDBECK

ABOUT THE VILLAGE

Named after the river (Cold-beck),
Caldbeck was a thriving rural
industrial centre before steam-power
and the Industrial Revolution. There is
still a clog-maker in the village centre.
In 1800 there were no fewer than
eight water-powered mills making
bobbins, woollens and grinding corn.

The Priests Mill which has been
beautifully restored houses a craft
centre, display area and restaurant
with a picture gallery. In the
churchyard is the famous Cumbrian
huntsman John Peel's grave, and that
of Mary, the Beauty of Buttermere
who was the subject of the novel 'The
Maid of Buttermere' by Melvyn Bragg.
Lord Bragg, incidentally, hails from
nearby Wigton and is understandably
proud of his local routes (he's a keen
cyclist).

 FOOD

PRIESTS MILL -
delicious vegetarian
food.
ODDFELLOWS
ARMS - pub food &
accommodation.

 POI

The Howk: beautiful
hidden pathway
through the woods to
a waterfall and the
aforementioned mill.
Take a break and have
a look...

The Clog Maker, Will
Strong: next to the
bridge.

185

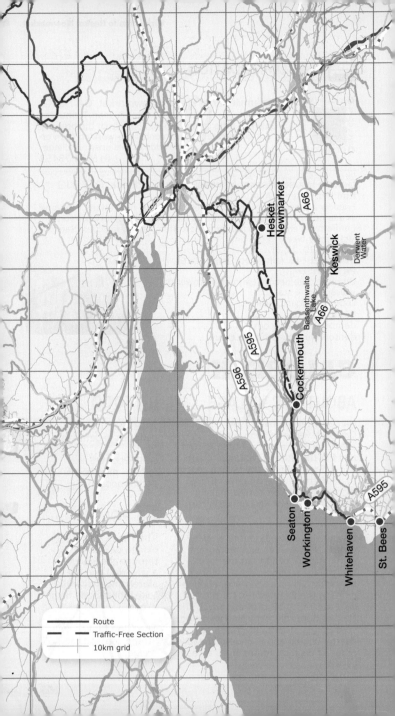

LONGLANDS → WHITEHAVEN

29 miles (8 miles traffic-free)

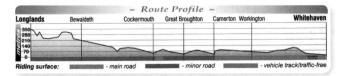

~ Route Profile ~

Longlands   Bewaldeth   Cockermouth   Great Broughton   Camerton Workington   **Whitehaven**

metres: 350 280 210 140 70 0

Riding surface: ▬▬ - main road   ▬▬ - minor road   ▬▬ - vehicle track/traffic-free

▶ ROUTE DESCRIPTION

- There are some steep bits as you emerge from Longlands, but once you get to Bewaldeth it is fairly easy riding into Cockermouth, a delightful stop-off for those who fancy a leisurely finish.
- Once you have passed Hewthwaite Hall (on your right) it is plain sailing into Cockermouth, where you arrive perilously close to the Jennings brewery.
- Those who can avoid such temptations might wish to push on to Workington or Whitehaven, the official finishing point. However, I find Cockermouth quite irresistible – fine ales, great fish and chips and one of the best vegetarian restaurants in Britain (the Quince & Medlar).
- One could quite easily undo all the benefits of several days hard cycling amongst such temptations.
- This is one of the most attractive towns in the northwest and is just outside the boundary of the Lake District National Park. Perhaps for this reason it is not inundated with tourists. It developed at the confluence of two great salmon rivers – the Cocker, which flows out of lakes Buttermere, Crummock and Loweswater; and the Derwent, which runs through lakes Derwent and Bassenthwaite to Workington.

- It has long fascinated writers, poets and artists and is the birthplace of William and Dorothy Wordsworth – one of the finest buildings here is Wordsworth House, the Lakeland poet's family home, which is now in the care of the National Trust.

COCKERMOUTH

✱ ← Full details in the C2C section of the guide: Page 43-46

▶ DIRECTIONS

- The route through Cockermouth differs from the C2C only in that you are heading from north to south, instead of vice versa (the detail map, right, has north at the bottom and south at the top).
- You arrive near Jennings Brewery and head up Main Street, passing the Tourist Information before taking a sharp right and heading towards Papcastle. There are plenty of things to
- do and lots of excellent places to eat and drink, which are covered in detail in the C2C section of this guide.

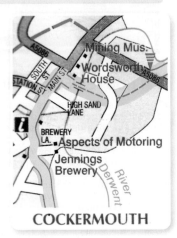

COCKERMOUTH

🛏 ACCOMMODATION

(← Full details in the C2C section of the guide: Page: 46)

Riverside, 12 Market St, Cumbria, CA13 9NJ, 01900 827504

Embleton Spa Hotel, Embleton, Near Cockermouth, CA13 9XU 017687 76606

WORKINGTON

✱ ← Full details in the C2C section of the guide: Pages 39-42

▶ DIRECTIONS

The road from Cockermouth to Workington follows the course of the Derwent via Papcastle, following the C2C in reverse, with the river on your left.

About 4km beyond Great Broughton is Camerton. At the Black Tom climb up to the right and at the old stone bridge hang a left onto the cycle track that takes you to Workington via Seaton. Again, be warned the map, right, shows the route coming in from the north, which is at the bottom.

ACCOMMODATION

(← Full details in the C2C section of the guide: Page 42)

Morven House Hotel, Siddick Rd, Workington, Cumbria CA14 1LE
01900 602118

Armidale Cottages, 29 High Seaton, CA14 1PD
01900 63704

Waverley Hotel 01900 65892

WHITEHAVEN

> ✱ ← Full details in the C2C section of the guide: Pages 27-31

▶ DIRECTIONS

The final stretch is pretty straightforward. You head out of Workington to Distington where you head for the coast, reaching it at the old Roman fort at Parton Bay and on to Whitehaven. Don't forget to dip your wheel in the briny.

ACCOMMODATION

(← Full details in the C2C section of the guide: Pages 30-31)

Chestnuts, Low Moresby, Whitehaven, Cumbria, CA28 6RX
01946 61612

Glenard Guest House, Inkerman Terr, Whitehaven, CA28 7TY
01946 692249

Chase Hotel, Inkerman Terrace, Whitehaven CA28 8AA
01946 693656

Moresby Hall, Moresby, Whitehaven, Cumbria, CA28 6PJ
01946 696317

Summergrove Halls, Hensingham, Whitehaven, CA28 8XZ,
01946 813328

Glenfield House, Low Corkickle, Whitehaven CA28 7TS
01946 691911

HADRIAN'S CYCLEWAY

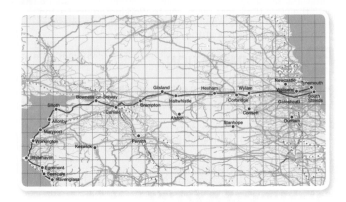

ABOUT HADRIAN'S CYCLEWAY

Hadrian's Cycleway is a 174 mile (280km) National Cycle Network route running through the World Heritage Site and the Solway Area of Outstanding Natural Beauty (AONB). Most of the route is well waymarked and open, and you can get a map and other useful pre-ride items from our website: hadrian-guide.co.uk.

For more background information take a look at the excellent website provided by Hadrian's Wall Heritage Ltd, the company set up to develop the economy of this World Heritage Site. hadrians-wall.org. The route was built by Sustrans, the UK's sustainable transport charity.

CYCLEWAY PROFILES

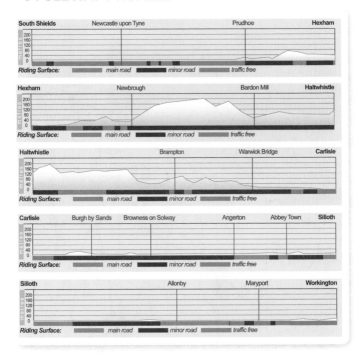

South Shields	Newcastle upon Tyne		Prudhoe	Hexham

Riding Surface: main road · minor road · traffic free

Hexham	Newbrough		Bardon Mill	Haltwhistle

Riding Surface: main road · minor road · traffic free

Haltwhistle		Brampton	Warwick Bridge	Carlisle

Riding Surface: main road · minor road · traffic free

Carlisle	Burgh by Sands	Browness on Solway	Angerton	Abbey Town	Silloth

Riding Surface: main road · minor road · traffic free

Silloth		Allonby	Maryport	Workington

Riding Surface: main road · minor road · traffic free

TYNEMOUTH & WHITLEY BAY
+ SOUTH SHIELDS → HEXHAM

Tynemouth to Hexham: 35 miles (mostly traffic-free)
South Shields to Hexham: 35 miles (mostly traffic-free)

TYNEMOUTH & WHITLEY BAY

Coast to host

We have pooled these two neighbouring communities so that those wishing to spend a night in the area have a better chance of finding a bed. Tynemouth is limited for accommodation but Whitley Bay abounds with it. The two towns form a significant cycle hub as they are at the beginning and end of several routes in addition to Hadrian's Cycleway: namely the C2C, Reivers and Coast & Castles.

Tynemouth, perched high above the North Sea, was a port in the time of Roman occupation and was used to supply troops manning Hadrian's Wall. Its ruined priory was built by monks from the Holy Island of Lindisfarne in the 7th century. Some 1,200 years later, in Victorian times, the area was filled by a new breed of holidaymaker who arrived on the newly built railway to enjoy the area's sheltered bathing and boating.

This is when Whitley Bay, with its Pleasure Dome, Spanish City and seaside villas, poked its head above the beach front. Whitley Bay is geared up for tourism. Every other building offers food, drink or accommodation - or all three. It is a strikingly traditional English seaside resort and is currently attempting to rediscover its former glory, when smart Geordies would jockey for space on the beach front.

WHERE TO EAT

GIORGIO'S PIZZERIA & RESTAURANT, Front St. 0191 257 3758
RENE'S, 22a Front St. Smart place, trendy & good food. 0191 257 0090
THE GATE OF INDIA, 40 Front St. 0191 258 3453
UNDAL, 3 Percy Park Road. 0191 257 8500
GIBRALTAR ROCK, East St. 0191 258 5655

Tynemouth Lodge Hotel, Tynemouth Rd, a real locals' pub frequented by the lifeboatmen. Great beers and often very busy. It's at the top of that steep climb out of the North Shields fish quays, on the edge of Tynemouth.

Hugo's, Front Street, is a handsome establishment. It is one of eight pubs in the small town. Has a changing selection of hand-pulled ales. Food served.

The Turks Head, Front St, otherwise known as the Stuffed Dog because of Willie the Scottish collie, whose 130 year old taxidermised remains sit in a glass box looking at the bar. Willie came down from the Scottish Borders with a herd of sheep and a shepherd, but somehow got separated from them and spent the rest of his life waiting and pining in Tynemouth for his lost master. A tale of epic proportions told in detail on a plaque. Good Courage Directors, regular guest ales. Food served all day.

POI

Tourist Information Centre
TICNS@northtyneside.gov.uk.
0191 200 5896 or 0191 200 8703

Sea Life Aquarium more than 30 hi-tech displays provide encounters with dozens of sea creatures. Journey 'beneath' the North Sea and discover thousands of amazing sea dwellers.

Black Middens once notorious rocks near the Tyne entrance which in the 1860s claimed five ships in three days. Tynemouth Castle and Priory: dating from the 7th century, this was the burial place for the Kings of Northumbria but was later destroyed by the Danes. Later founded as a Benedictine Priory and later still fortified, but now a picturesque ruin.

BIKE SHOPS

Whiptail Cycles
3, Livingston View,
Tynemouth, Tyne & Wear,
NE30 2PL
0191 257 2212

Dixons Cycles
184 Park View,Whitley
Bay,Tyne and Wear,
NE26 3QP.
info@dixons-cycles.co.uk
0191 253 2035

ACCOMMODATION

The Metropolitan, 13 Esplanade, Whitley Bay, NE26 2AH

Run by: Andrew Stephenson & Stephen Dodds

Sleeps up to 24 so is ideal for groups. Contemporary 4-star B&B on the quiet area of Whitley Bay, but only a couple of minutes walk from the award-winning beach and short stroll to the vibrant town centre. Highly recommended on all review sites and currently voted the the top place to stay in Tyne & Wear on Tripadvisor. Free wireless internet throughout, all rooms are en-suite and the room facilities include 32" LCD TV, iPod dock, radio alarm clock, DVD player, Freeview, complimentary hospitality tray, luxury toiletries and towels. Free on-street parking.

Rooms: 1S, 3T, 1D, 1F (sleeps up to six) plus pop-up beds.
B&B: from £35 (£30 if sharing family room). £45 single occ.
Eve meal: no, but lots of choice nearby.
Pk lunch: by arrangement. Secure lock up. Drying facilities.
0191 253 4941
info@themetropolitan.co
themetropolitan.co

▶ DIRECTIONS

- Take good note: it is easy to get lost beyond North Shields. Start at the Spanish Battery Car Park by the cluster of arty waysigns below the Castle and Priory. Leaving Admiral Collingwood's fine statue on your right follow the cycle path to North Shields Fish Quays with its restaurants, fish and chip shops and old fashioned stores.

- There is a plethora of Route 72, Route 10 and C2C signs (you are also on the C2C). Union Quay becomes Bell St, Liddle St and Clive St. Follow the signs, which take you to Lowson St. At the end of Chirton Dene Way you need to skirt round to the right of Wet n'Wild indoor water park.

- Follow the path to the right, along the cycle path parallel with Coble Dene, opposite the shopping centre at Royal Quays, where the DFDS ferries come in. Turn left onto the cycle path following the busy A187. Take care when crossing it. A clearly delineated cycle path shortly takes you above the Tyne, past Segedunum Roman Baths & Museum, skirting Wallsend, Walker and Byker before you are reunited with the Tyne and the magnificent run into Newcastle.

Fish Quay is a vibrant little community of retailers who inhabit this scenic stretch. There are a couple of good pubs and plenty of places to eat, all commanding views of the Tyne. This is where Danish and Polish sailors used to come ashore to integrate vigorously with the local community at a den of iniquity known as the Infamous Jungle (this former brothel is now known as the Collingwood Buildings).

SOUTH SHIELDS

Changing face of Tyneside

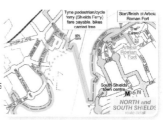

South Shields has six miles of coastline and three miles of river frontage, dominated by the massive piers at the mouth of the Tyne. One of the most striking features of South Shields (home of the romantic author Catherine Cookson) is its Town Hall of 1910, with its copper weather vane in the form of a galleon. Airships raided the Tyne in World War I and the town's seafront amusement park was attacked in 1915. In World War II, it was much targeted by the Germans (156 people were killed in air raids). One direct hit on the market place killed more than 40 people who had taken shelter in tunnels below the square. South Shields also lost more seafarers than any other port in Britain during World War II.

The celebrated artist L S Lowry spent frequent periods at the Seaburn Hotel in Sunderland, and painted a number of works in South Shields. The town has also been home to a Yemeni community since the 1890s.

In 1977 it was visited by boxer Muhammad Ali, whose wedding was blessed in the local mosque at Laygate. Ali visited the town after receiving an invitation from a local boys' boxing club.

South Shields has undergone significant post-industrial economic change. The shipyards, mines, salt pans and glass making have been replaced by service industries, including tourism and retail.

197

📕 PLACES OF INTEREST

Tourist Information Centre, Museum & Gallery, Ocean Rd, South Shields, NE33 2HZ. 0191 454 6612

Those interested in history will wish to have a good look at the supply base at **Arbeia Roman Fort & Museum.** Reconstructions, Life of a Roman Soldier exhibition and Death & Burial gallery are all part of this hands-on exhibition to show what it was like for the ordinary Roman soldier.
Open April 1 – Oct 31 1000-1700; Nov 1 – March 31 1000-1500 daily. Admission: FREE. 0191 456 1369
twmuseums.org.uk/arbeia.

Tyne Cycle Tunnel
The tunnel was opened in 1951 to service the shipyards and was once used by 20,000 people a day. The tunnel is 274 metres long and was the first purpose-built cycle tunnel. Tiled in elegant green and white, there is a red brick rotunda at each end and a distinct flavour of the recent industrial past. As it is a public highway, the tunnel is free and is open 24 hours a day. There is also a lift should the old escalator be out of service.

Bede's World, Church Bank, Jarrow, Tyne & Wear, NE32 3DY
If you're taking your time (and we feel that you should), Bede's World (right) is well worth a visit. It is a lively celebration of the extraordinary life of the Venerable Bede (AD 673-735), who lived here 1300 years ago. The museum, next to the Tyne, has changing exhibitions. There's a good café in Jarrow Hall and a new museum building.
0191 489 2106
F: 0191 428 2361
info@bedesworld.co.uk
bedesworld.co.uk

PUBS

Alum Ale House, River Drive, NE33 1JR. Next to the ferry terminal. Claims to be the oldest pub in South Shields. But so does The Steamboat in Coronation St. 0191 427 7147.

The Maltings, Claypath Lane, NE33 4PG. One of the three pubs owned by Jarrow Brewery. Big and welcoming. 0191 427 7147.

St Mary's Lighthouse

Stag's Head, 45 Fowler St, NE33 1NS. Every Thursday there's a curry night. It costs £1. The pub has an award for its unchanged interior. It should get one for its prices. 0191 427 2911.

The Steamboat, Coronation St, Mill Dam, NE33 1EQ. Overlooks the Tyne (rather than the sea). Community pub. Claims to be the oldest in South Shields (see Alum above). 0191 454 0134.

 BIKE SHOPS

A-S Cycles 44 St Aidans Road, South Shields NE33 2HD
Tel: 0191 456 3133

Conway Cycle Centre 12 Salem Street, South Shields, Tyne and Wear NE33 1HH Tel: 0191 455 3579

Halfords Station Road, Millbank, South Shields, Tyne & Wear, NE33 1ED. Tel: 0191 4271600

- If you opt for South Shields as opposed to Tynemouth the official start point is at Arbeia Roman Fort. However, many might wish to start at the mouth of the Tyne, just a mile or so east at Littlehaven Beach, where there are wonderful views of the harbour and Tynemouth Priory. The sandy beach is home to The Conversation Piece, a highly unusual work of art, next to the Littlehaven Hotel. Leaving the rotund sculptures behind, head up the gentle incline towards Arbeia, following the Tyne as it briefly courses southwards.

- If you wish to see the Arbeia replica fort you need to head up River Drive then left again and briefly into Mile End Road, turning sharp left into Green Place, then right into Baring St. Retrace your steps down to Wapping Street and head west along the Tyne, not forgetting to take in the wonderful views. You will pass the Spirit of the Tyne statue and the dry dock.

- Follow the signs and you will soon be at South Shields ferry crossing (£1.10 – bikes free for a seven minute crossing at 15 and 45 minutes past the hour) should you wish to opt for the route along North Tyneside.

- Otherwise, simply carry on until Jarrow and cross at the Cycle Tunnel, next to Bede's World. This is a mostly urban section but with some good views across the Tyne before you reach the path next to the A194. You follow the main road for about a mile before taking a right turn just before Jarrow (clearly waysigned). You will be passing the ruined monastery of St Paul on the right before taking a left past Bede's World.

- This is where you should cross the Tyne, via the tunnel. There is a designated cycle tunnel running parallel with the pedestrian tunnel and the world's longest wooden escalator takes you down into the depths of the earth (60 metres). You link up with the route the other side, near Howdon Metro. The more people who use the tunnel, the more likely it is to stay open!

- You will now be linked up with the North Tyneside section of the route. For instructions (in the unlikely event you get lost), please see Tynemouth – Newcastle section.

NEWCASTLE

Ancient 21st century Toon

Newcastle is far from new:
its origins are Roman.
It owes its name to the
castle built in 1080 by
Robert, eldest son of
William the Conqueror.
Wool was its business
before coal took over.
It became a port in the
16th century and soon
shipyards lower down the
river were established,
later to become amongst
the world's largest build
and repair centres. In
these post-industrial times
the city is largely business
and culture led, with a
particular reputation for nightlife.

The medieval street layout still exists in large parts of the
centre, with narrow alleys or 'chares', particularly around the
riverside area. There are steps leading up from the Tyne to
higher parts of the city and the Castle Keep, whose existence

was first recorded in the 14th century. Close, Sandhill and Quayside boast some fine modern architecture alongside older buildings dating from 15th-18th centuries. These include Bessie Surtees' House, the Cooperage and Lloyds Quayside Bars, Derwentwater House and the wonderful listed 16th century merchant's house at 28-30 Close.

Its late Georgian neoclassical centre, built in the early 19th century by John Dobson, has been restored in recent years and vies with Bath for period splendour. Newcastle has been described as England's best-looking city and Grey Street, which curves down from Grey's Monument towards the valley of the Tyne, was voted England's finest street in a survey of Radio 4 listeners. Sadly a section of Grainger Town was bulldozed in the 1960s to make way for the shopping centre at Eldon Square.

Leazes Park, northwest of the centre, was built in 1873 as a *'ready access to some open ground for the purpose of health and recreation'* following a petition by 3,000 working men. Adjoining the park is St James's Park, home of Newcastle United, which dominates many views of the city.

🔭 PLACES OF INTEREST

Tourist Information Centre: Guildhall Visitor Information Centre, Quayside, NE1 3AF. 0191 277 8000, newcastle.gov.uk

8-9 Central Arcade, NE1 5BQ, 0191 277 8000

Segedunum Roman Fort, Baths & Museum

At Wallsend, just east of the city. This is a spectacular reconstruction of a fort which includes the bath house and a section of the wall, also offering a computer generated history tour and a 35 metre high viewing tower.
Open April 1 – Oct 31 1000-1700; Nov 1 – March 31 1000-1500 daily. Adults: £3.95, concessions £2.95. U-16s free.
0191 236 9347.
twmuseums.org.uk/segedunum.

BIKE SHOPS

Cycle Centre 248 Shields Road Byker Newcastle upon Tyne
Tyne & Wear, NE6 1DX.
0191 265 1472 sales@cyclecentreuk.co.uk, cyclecentre.co.uk

Cycle Logical
44 Forest Hall Road, Forest Hall. Newcastle upon Tyne - Tyne and
Wear, NE12 9AL 0191 216 9222, cyclelogical-newcastle.com

Denton Cycles, 259 Scotswood Rd, NE4 7AW, Tel: 0191 272 338

Edinburgh Bicycle Cooperative, 5-7 Union Road, Byker,
NE6 1EH
0191 265 8619, edinburgh-bicycle.co.uk (N.B. Formerly known
as Hardisty's) 1 mile north of NCN 72 - via Byker Link and Shields
Road

Recyke Y'Bike, Hannington Street, Byker, NE6 1JT
A community project that accepts donated bikes from members
of the public and recycles them for use by priority groups of
people, such as the long-term unemployed, those who have been
homeless, and those with mental health problems.
Contact: Dorothy Craw.
07737 526020 F: 0191 292 9963, recyke-y-bike.org

 # ACCOMMODATION

The Cumberland Arms, Ouseburn, Byker, Newcastle upon
Tyne, Tyne & Wear, NE6 1LD
A traditional, vibrant community pub with four beautiful en-suite
rooms, all with super king size beds. Ideally placed to explore the
city or you could choose to settle in and enjoy with its open fires,
real ale and cider, and a variety of music to listen to. The food menu
is not to be missed with everything from pie, chips & mushy peas to
pork belly & mash, we also do a cracking Sunday Dinner! Featured by
Oz Clarke and James May on TV, described in Lonely Planet magazine
by the former as one of the 'best pubs I've ever been in.'
Rooms: 4D/T.
B&B: D/T £80, S £70, Family £100 (inc continental b'fast).
Opening hours: 3pm - 11pm Mon, Tues,
Thurs & Sun; and 3pm -12am Wed, Fri & Sat.
Food served: 3pm - 8pm.
Packed lunch: £5
Secure cycle storage. Drying facilities.
0191 265 1725 \ 0191 265 6151
info@thecumberlandarms.co.uk
thecumberlandarms.co.uk

NEWCASTLE → WYLAM/OVINGHAM

- As you head out of the city with the urban sprawl of Elswick and Benwell on your right, gradually the countryside opens up. Watch out for fishermen blocking the path. At mile point 161 you will need to cross the busy Scotswood Road onto its north side, soon joining the rail path, only to cross back again two miles later, around the point where the C2C branches off for Rowlands Gill. Carry on towards Newburn, closely following the (well signposted) Tyne along a flat section.

- Soon you will be passing just south of Heddon on the Wall, a pleasant little village bang on Hadrian's Wall. This is worth a stop off as there is an excellent B&B and The Swan does a good and cheap carvery.

🍴 WHERE TO EAT

THE SWAN, Reliable and copious carvery. Other options in a neatly refurbished old pub.
01661 853161

▶ ROUTE DESCRIPTION

Just before Wylam you cross onto the south side of the Tyne at Hagg Bank until Ovingham, crossing bank onto the north bank at Prudhoe railway station. Please note that there is no cycling on the footbridge and be careful on the road bridge as it's narrow and dangerous.

Take care on narrow bridge, loop back under bridge to join riverside path

WYLAM & PRUDHOE

Steam makes way for pedal power

The loss of the Scotswood, Newburn and Wylam Railway was the cyclist's gain: the HCW follows its course before taking you through this picturesque Tyneside community, with its own splendid little brewery. Wylam was the home of George Stephenson, 'father of the railway', and his cottage is now a bijou museum. The old line, needless to say, ran past its doorway. On the opposite side of the river the Tyne Valley Railway still operates between Newcastle and Carlisle.

Wylam has also been home to the novelists Margaret Drabble, Lady Antonia (A.S.) Byatt, not to mention the former BBC boss Greg Dyke. Charles Algernon Parsons, inventor of the steam turbine, lived here, as did rail pioneers William Hedley and Timothy Hackworth. It has benefited – as has the entire Tyne Valley – from the recent prosperity of Newcastle.

🏛 PLACES OF INTEREST

Wylam Railway Museum, Falcon Centre, Falcon Tce, Wylam, NE41 8EE. Closed for refurbishment Opening hours may be limited. 01661 852174

George Stephenson's Birthplace, Wylam NE41 8BP. 19/3/09 – 1/11/09 1200-1700 Thurs, Fri, Sat & Sun plus Bank Holiday Mondays. £2 adults £1 children. 01661 853457

Wormald House & local shop: 01661 852529
wormaldhouse.co.uk

Bistro-en-Glaze, restaurant with rooms: 01661 852185

Winships, Prudhoe – traditional English cooking, fish fresh from North Shields and locally reared meat. Chef/proprietor Keith Jarvis. 01661 835099. winships.co.uk.

OVINGHAM ➜ CORBRIDGE

Never mind that Hadrian's Wall is a few miles to the north at this point. Roman troops would not have had anything like as good a view of the Tyne. Cross over Ovingham Bridge and hang a left into River View, going past the local school. You are now on the country lane that takes you north of Bywell, just past mile marker 148, going under the A68 near Riding Mill. There is a mile long climb here taking you from Styford Bridge past High Barns. The lane then takes you to a T-junction, where you head left and descend into Corbridge.

Tynemouth as seen from the Littlehaven start point.

CORBRIDGE

Potted history

Corbridge is not just a pretty face, it is a real place. One of the most attractive towns in the north of England, it bustles with activity. Its name probably derives from the Roman 'coria', which means 'tribal centre'. Lying at the junction of Stanegate and Dere Street, it was a major Roman stronghold. The fort here was established in AD 85 and by the middle of the 2nd century a town, with two walled military compounds, had grown around it. Some spectacular finds have been unearthed, including the Corbridge Lion and the Corbridge Hoard of Armour.

The parish church of St Andrew was consecrated in 676 and the first bridge across this broad and fast flowing stretch of the Tyne was built in the 13th century, though the current seven-arched structure dates from 1674. Corbridge, like many towns in the area, suffered during the border warfare in the area from the 14th century. Marauders, known as Reivers, behaved much like a completely unrestrained version of the Sicilian mafia (see Reivers section for gory details). Border warfare, at its height between 1300 and 1550, continued in one form or another for an unconscionable total of 400 years.

Having mentioned writers connected with Wylam I feel duty bound to do credit to Corbridge: the town boasts (in addition to South Shields) Catherine Cookson and Ruth Ainsworth, frequent contributor to 'Listen with Mother'.

🔭 PLACES OF INTEREST

For background: hadrians-wall.org. 01434 322002

Tourist Information Centre, Hill St (Easter until end of October). 01434 632815

Corbridge Roman Town (0.5 miles north west of Corbridge). Substantial remains. Granaries, a stone lion and the Stanegate Road. All comes to life with an audio tour. Open all year round. Admission: £4.50, concessions £3.60, children £2.10.
01434 632349
english-heritage.org.uk/corbridge

◉ Bike Shops

Activcycles, 17 Watling St Corbridge
info@activcycles.net
activcycles.net

WHERE TO EAT

THE CORBRIDGE LARDER – Deli and coffee shop. Cavernous and copious. 01434 632948. www. corbridgelarder.co.uk

WATLING COFFEE HOUSE, 11 Watling St, NE45 5AG. Smart but slightly offbeat hangout for those requiring anything from a coffee to a full meal. 01434 634820.

TEA & TIPPLE, Market Place, NE45 5AW. Opposite the ancient church and popular with shoppers. 01434 632886.

CORBRIDGE → HEXHAM

- Follow the one way system through Middle St and you will soon pass the Corbridge Roman site. It's only four miles to Hexham. Watch out for fast traffic joining and leaving the A69. Just beyond Anick the lane can get busy with commuter and industrial traffic. You should dismount to cross the busy road bridge into Hexham.

HEXHAM

Potted history

Hexham has just over 11,000 people and is one of the three major towns in Tynedale (along with Prudhoe and Haltwhistle). The town's beginnings lie in the establishment of a monastery by Saint Wilfrid in 674. The crypt of the original monastery survives, and incorporates many stones taken from nearby Roman ruins. Hexham Abbey dates mainly from the 11th century, but was significantly rebuilt in Victorian times. Other notable buildings in the town include the Moot Hall, the covered market, and the Old Gaol.

Like Corbridge and many other towns in the North of England, Hexham had its nose bloodied on many occasions during the border wars with the Scots. Amongst those to administer them was William Wallace, who burnt the town in 1297, though the abbey survived largely intact. Not to be outdone Robert the Bruce demanded (and got) a ransom of £2,000 some 15 years later, in 1312, in exchange for not burning it down.

During the Wars of the Roses Hexham was the scene of battle in 1464. The Duke of Somerset, who commanded the Lancastrians, was defeated and beheaded in the Market Place. Later the town played its part in the 1715 Jacobite uprising, when James Radclyffe, 3rd Earl of Derwentwater, raised the standard on behalf of the Stuarts. For his pains he was beheaded after the battle of Preston.

PLACES OF INTEREST

Tourist Information Centre, Wentworth Car Park, Hexham NE46 1QE. 01434 652220. ukinformationcentre.com (then type in Hexham).

Further information: hadrians-wall.org. 01434 322002.

Hexham Abbey: the current Early English Gothic church largely dates from c.1170–1250. The choir, north and south transepts and the cloisters, where canons studied and meditated, date from this period. The east end was rebuilt in 1860.
The Abbey stands at the west end of the market place, which is home to the Shambles, a Grade II* covered market built in 1766 by Sir Walter Blackett.

Moot Hall: a 15th century building in the east of the market place, is Grade I listed but not open to the public as it is home of the museum department of Tynedale District Council!
Old Gaol: one of the first purpose built prisons in England, it was constructed in 1330 and is a Grade I listed Scheduled Monument. Commissioned by the Archbishop of York (clerics were also governors and warriors in these times). There is now a museum.

 ## BIKE SHOPS

The Bike Shop
16-17, St. Marys Chare Hexham Northumberland
01434 601032

 # WHERE TO EAT

SAATHI INDIAN RESTAURANT & TAKEAWAY, 28 Priestpopple. With a growing reputation, much more restaurant than curry house. 01434 603509

BOUCHON BISTROT, 4-6 Gilesgate. French, and excellent quality and value from reports.
01434 609943
bouchonbistrot.co.uk

WALL

Out of Hexham and a couple of miles up the A6079 road towards Chollerford, and the famous Chesters Bridge Abutment, is the Hadrian Hotel at Wall. This is a splendid pitstop, with excellent real ales and good cooking. You can link up with the route just beyond Chollerford and Walwick.

ACCOMMODATION

Hadrian Hotel, Wall, Hexham, NE46 4EE.
Run by: David Lindsay
Comfortable and cosy without being remotely stuffy. As a guest you can hunker down in front of the fire or go and have a beer in the lively public bar. The food is well executed and reasonably priced and the rooms are very comfortable without being expensive. A class operation at an affordable price.
Rooms: 2D, 4T.
B&B: £32-£44.
Evening meal: from £7-£17.
Pk lunch: £7.95
Secure lock-up and drying facilities.
01434 681232
david.lindsay13@btinternet.com
hadrianhotel.co.uk

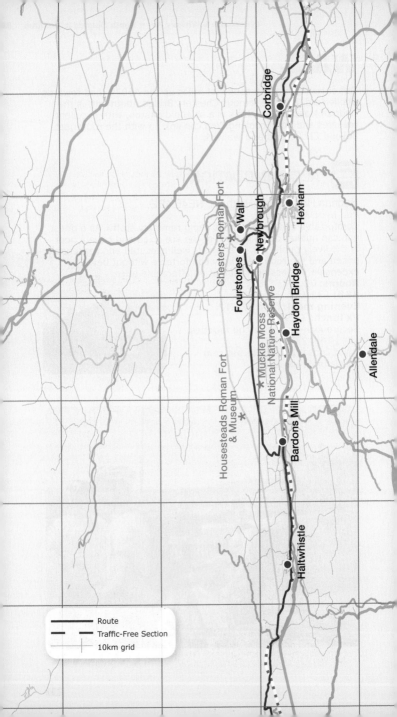

Corbridge

Wall

Chesters Roman Fort

Newbrough

Hexham

Fourstones

Haydon Bridge

Muckle Moss
National Nature Reserve

Allendale

Housesteads Roman Fort
& Museum

Bardons Mill

Haltwhistle

Route
Traffic-Free Section
10km grid

HEXHAM → HALTWHISTLE

22 miles (0 miles traffic-free)

▶ DIRECTIONS

- There are two gated level crossings as you exit the town. Take care. You can also go directly to Fourstones but this is a narrow lane and therefore potentially hazardous as there are no verges. Instead, at mile marker 137, head up past Thistlerigg Farm. This takes you to Chesters Roman Fort, which is well worth a stop and is about one mile further than the left turn onto the B6319 which takes you down to Fourstones.

> Mid-way between mile marker 130 and 129, at Grindon Hill where the Haydon Bridge lane connects with the Military Road, is a splendid and isolated stop-off.

▶ DIRECTIONS

- If not going to Chesters, turn left onto the B6319 and head down to Fourstones and be prepared: the steepest climbing is about to start along the Stanegate (old Roman road), once you get to Newbrough. There's a 200 metre ascent to the highest point on the route, Crindledykes (262 metres).

- A two mile diversion ahead takes you to Housesteads Roman Fort (Vercovicivm). For background: hadrians-wall.org. 01434 322002. A little further (steeply) down the route and then back up an equally steep section is Vindolanda fort. Tea room and museum. Easier and quicker to access than Housesteads.

- You are in the heart of Roman Britain. You will also see signs for Route 68 at Smith's Shield. This where Pennine Cycleway and HCW conjoin. There is now a steep descent to Bardon Mill, where you go under the A69 before turning right.

HALTWHISTLE

Potted history
Haltwhistle comes
from Old English words
Hal-twysel, meaning 'a
meeting of the streams
by the hill'. Twistle is a
meeting of the waters
and here the Haltwhistle
Burn from the north meets
the River South Tyne,
thus making it a strategic

settlement for the Romans. The Wall is just over half a mile to
the north, and much of the stone was quarried nearby.
On the Newcastle to Carlisle rail line, the town developed with
the industrial revolution. In the 18th and 19th centuries coal
mining was the main industry. Metal ores extracted from the
mines on Alston Moor were also loaded here.
In 1836 workmen found a copper vessel containing 63 gold and
copper coins with the minted heads of four Emperors: Claudius
Caesar; Nero Claudius Drusus Germanicus; Nero and Vespasian.
More recently, paint manufacture became a major commercial
force in the town, but has now stopped major production. In
the 21st century, the tourist industry dominates the economy,
with Hadrian's Wall and walking and cycling counting among the
principal interests of tourists.

Places of Interest

Tourist Information Centre, Railway Station, Station Rd.
01434 322002

Church of the Holy Cross, below the Market Place with views
over the river and the valley. 13th century and impressive for a
modest town. Medieval graves.

Cycle shops

Edens Lawn Cycle
Hire, By Pass Road,
Haltwhistle, NE49
0HH
01434 320443

THIS ONE
RUNS ON FAT
AND SAVES YOU MONEY

THIS ONE
RUNS ON MONEY
AND MAKES YOU FAT

Featherstone Castle near Haltwhistle

Route

Traffic-Free Section

10km grid

Haltwhistle

Alston

Gilsland

A69

Lanercost
Priory

Brampton

Carlisle

A7

HALTWHISTLE → CARLISLE

29 miles (mostly on-road)

HALTWHISTLE → GILSLAND (5 MILES)

GILSLAND

Potted history

Most of the 400 inhabitants live on the Northumberland side of the Poltross Burn and the River Irthing. Gilsland Spa has been a popular tourist attraction and there is a Spa Hotel, owned by the Cooperative Society. Sir Walter Scott visited in 1797 and later popularised it. After a whirlwind courtship with French émigrée, Margaret Charlotte Charpentier, Scott is said to have proposed at the Popping Stone. They married in December 1797.

Gilsland, originally an Iron Age settlement, has Milecastle 48 on its doorstep. Farming and mining were its staple businesses but now tourism (courtesy of the Wall) has taken over. Some 100 of the local inhabitants earn part or all their living from tourism and there are plenty of B&Bs.

 Places of Interest

Tourist Information Centre: 01697 747211

St Mary Magdalene's Church is set in beautiful rural surroundings. Early English Gothic style. Built and partially endowed by George Gill Mounsey who also erected what is now the Gilsland Spa Hotel.

Gilsland Spa, known in the past for its sulphurous spa waters, is close by.

▶ ROUTE DESCRIPTION

Follow the B6318 for just over a mile before turning left at Kiln Hill. This will take you past Birdoswald Fort. You will follow a three mile section of wall down to Banks Turret. There are great views to be had before heading down past Lanercost Priory (well worth a visit – there's a café and conveniences). Brampton is a further 3.5 miles.

BRAMPTON

Potted History

One of the bigger conurbations, some 4,000 people live in this handsome sandstone enclave which nestles in a hollow gouged out during the ice age. There are several striking features to the town, among them St Martin's Church, famous as the only place of worship designed by the Pre-Raphaelite architect Philip Webb. St Martin's contains one of the most exquisite sets of stained glass windows designed by Sir Edward Burne-Jones, and executed in the William Morris studio.

On the outskirts of Brampton lies the Old Parish Church built, like so many edifices in the area, from Hadrian's Wall stone. In use until St Martin's was built in 1878, only the chancel now remains. Another fine feature is the octagonal Moot Hall, built in 1817. The Moot Hall has an external staircase to its upper entrance, pointed windows and a square turret. The building now houses the Tourist Information Centre. East of the town is an exceptionally large motte, about 135 feet high on top of which is a statue of the 7th Earl of Carlisle.

🔭 PLACES OF INTEREST

Tourist Information Centre, Moot House. 016977 3433.

Lanercost Priory is an absolute must, a romantic gem built in the reign of Henry II in around 1166. When completed in 1220, canons came from the priory in Norfolk. It was unceremoniously decommissioned by Henry VIII during the Dissolution of the Monasteries.

⚙ BIKE SHOPS

Pedal Pushers
Lonnings End, Lonning, Capontree Road, Brampton, Cumbria, CA8 1QL
016977 42387 | pedalpushersbram@aol.com

▶ BRAMPTON → CARLISLE (15 MILES)

▶ ROUTE DESCRIPTION

Pretty straightforward. You may wish to take the short cut to Warwick Bridge at Hayton. Otherwise follow the signs. HCW takes you through Newby East, Newby Grange and the attractive hamlet of Crosby-on-Eden, four miles east of Carlisle.

CROSBY-ON-EDEN

This delightful hamlet on the banks of the river Eden is a rural overnight alternative to Carlisle for those wishing to avoid staying in busy towns and cities. There's a cracking little pub serving good food and well kept beer.

Crosby-on-Eden is in fact two tiny parishes combined – Low Crosby and High Crosby, joined by the Stanegate Roman road. It is close to General Wade's 18th century military road which goes across northern England. During World War II many Hurricane pilots were trained at RAF Crosby-on-Eden, as well as the Bristol Beaufort night fighters.

A lovely hidden gem, bypassed by the busy 21st century. You could easily miss it. Be warned!

🍴 WHERE TO EAT

Stag Inn, Low Crosby, Crosby-on-Eden, Cumbria
Strategically placed pub serving food all day, every day. Normal pub grub during the day before morphing into a gastropub of an evening. Wide and eclectic range - mezzes and other Med cuisine, North African tagines, spicy prawns cooked Indian style - the range is impressive, the portions generous and the prices more in tune with pubs than astro-gastro.
01228 573210

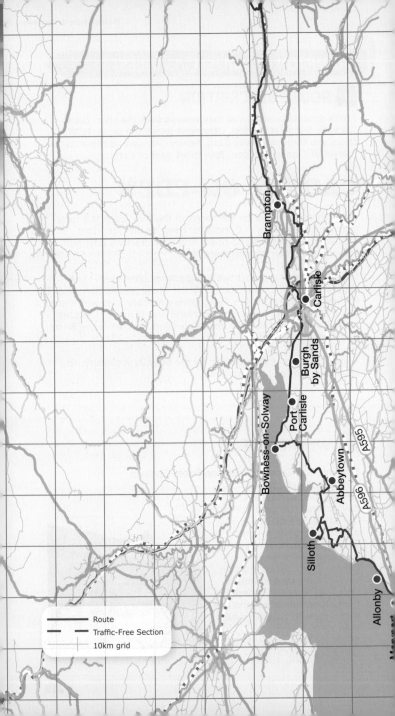

CARLISLE ➜ SILLOTH

35 miles (mostly on-road)

CARLISLE

Potted history

These days Carlisle greets its guests with open arms, but not so long ago any visitor would have been treated with suspicion. It was the nerve-centre for bitter feuds and bloody battles created by the disputed Border. Early in its history it was a Roman headquarters for the Wall. In 1092 William the Conqueror's son William Rufus started to build the castle where later Mary Queen of Scots was incarcerated. During a period of Scots occupation its ruler was one Macbeth. Known as 'Carluel' it was, according to legend, the domain of King Arthur, and the Emperor Hadrian was perhaps the first to realize that whoever held Carlisle could influence the destinies of both England and Scotland.

You only have to look at the vast ramparts of the castle to realise the city's strategic importance. It is the home today of the King's Own Royal Border Regimental museum. If you get time, it is worth looking at its labyrinths to find the Licking Stones, so called because the water running down them was the only form of sustenance available to the Jacobite prisoners captured following Bonnie Prince Charlie's retreat in December 1745. The cathedral is also worth a visit. The city's long-running commercial success is celebrated in the Guildhall Museum, once a meeting place of the medieval trade guilds. Home of Carr's biscuits, its pubs were once nationalised to regulate drinking hours because of the massive (and dangerous) munitions industry which dominated the local economy.

PLACES OF INTEREST

Tourist Information Centre, Old Town Hall, Green Market, Carlisle CA3 8JA. 01228 625600

If by chance you have cycled all the way from Wallsend and still need to know more about the Roman history of the Wall then before you leave Carlisle it is worth visiting Tullie House. This excellent museum will also give you a great deal of local information to help you on your way.

 ## CYCLE SHOPS

Hollymill Cycles 140 Botchergate, Carlisle, CA1 1SH.
01228 513909

Palace Cycles 120 - 124 Botchergate, Carlisle, CA1 1SH
01228 523142

Rickerby's Currock Road, Carlisle, CA2 4BL
01228 27521

Scotby Cycles, 1 Church Street, Caldewgate, Carlisle, CA2 5TL
01228 546931

Whitehead Cycle Centre 128 - 130 Botchergate, Carlisle, CA1 1SH
01228 526890

 ## ACCOMMODATION

Hazeldean Guest House, Orton Grange, Wigton Road, Carlisle, Cumbria CA5 6JB

Run by: Susan Harper

Friendly guest house with a unique attraction, 50m from Hadrian route: complementary therapies available - massage, reflexology and reiki. Spa suite, hot tub and sauna so ideal for an exhausted cyclist. Large garden, secure parking for bikes.

Rooms: 1S, 2D, 1T.
B&B: £30.
Pk lunch: from £4.
Eve meal: £7-£10.
On route. VisitBritain 3 stars.
Pub: nearby.
01228 711953
hazeldean1@btopenworld.com
hazeldeantherapycentre.com

Crown & Mitre Hotel, English Street, Carlisle, Cumbria CA3 8HZ
Run by: Duty Manager
This splendid Edwardian hotel was built in 1905 on the site of
the original Crown and Mitre Inn. There's a blazing log fire in the
lobby and 25 rooms have been refurbished, with five of them now
containing the full Sky package. It also has a family suite with
a Playstation 3 and can take a family of 5 people. The swimming
pool has also been fully re-furbished. The Crown & Mitre really
welcomes cyclists and is a truly comfortable and stylish place to
take a night off and rest your weary limbs. Great for groups.
Rooms: 16S, 78 D/T.
B&B: £40pp (single supplement £20).
Secure cycle storage.
Excellent restaurant serving a wide variety of meals.
01228 525491
info@crownandmitre-hotel-carlisle.com
crownandmitre-hotel-carlisle.com

Langleigh Guest House, 6 Howard Place, Carlisle, CA1 1HR
Run by: Yvette Rogers
Warm tastefully decorated Victorian house in a quiet conserva-
tion area with private car park and only five minutes walk from
the city centre. Tea and coffee making facilities and flat screen
TVs. Laundry & Drying facilities; secure lockable storage for
bikes and equipment. Evening Meals and packed lunches avail-
able. Ideal place to stop for on the first night if you've set off
from Ravenglass and don't mind a long day in the saddle!
Rooms: 1S, 3D, 3T, 1F
B&B: S £40. D £75. Tpl £110.
Pk lunch: £5.50.
Eve meal: £8-£25 (BYOB)
VisitBritain: 4 stars
Pub: 5 minutes
Lock-up/drying facilities
01228 530440
langleighhouse@aol.com
langleighhouse.co.uk

Old Brewery Residences, Bridge Lane, Caldewgate, Carlisle CA2 5SR

Run by: Dee Carruthers

Accommodation in Youth Hostel rooms. All single rooms in self catering flats of 7 bedrooms. Also excellent cycle shop 5 mins walk along road. No meals available on site. But only 5 mins walk from town centre - with plenty of cafes/restaurants and supermarkets. The Old Brewery is part of the Old Theakstons Brewery and sits beside the River Caldew, opposite Carlisle Castle, and is a student hall of residence for most of the year converting into a youth hostel during the summer months.

Rooms: 7 - 56 beds.

Rates: £24 (£20 for u-18s)

01228 597352
deec@impacthousing.org.uk
impacthousing.org.uk

LEAVING CARLISLE

▶ ROUTE DESCRIPTION

The start of the next phase of your journey is along the
close planted borders of Castle Park. Enjoy these tree-lined
avenues because soon you will be out on the open marshes
and completely exposed to sun and wind for mile after mile.
You cross the River Caldew by a bridge built on the line of the
Roman Wall. Just around the bend of the river a new bridge over
the River Eden is
planned, which will
become the start
of NCN Route 7 to
Scotland.

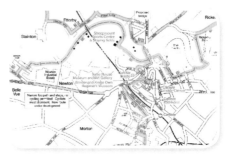

Beyond the second
railway viaduct is
a steep flight of
steps which leads
you up to the area
known as Engine
Lonning, whose
ruinous ramblings
hide a fascinating history. The wall ran just a few metres from
the top of the steps. In 1823 the Castle Canal was opened from
its basin here to Port Carlisle giving the merchants of the city
a route to Liverpool. In 1853 the canal was drained and filled
in by the Port Carlisle Railway Company. From here you have
a virtually level journey for the next 87 miles all the way to
Ravenglass.

The first part of the cycle route runs along the edge of the
railway cutting, which is now even more filled in, but there are
hopes to extend
the route along
the railway for
another mile or
now that the new
Carlisle bypass
has opened.
You join the
road through
Knockupworth
and follow roads
all the way to the
Maryport Golf
Club, 47 miles
away.

BURGH BY SANDS

Potted history

Burgh by Sands has numerous Roman remains. This was a vital strategic point, where troops were stationed to guard the two nearby Solway fords which were used by Scottish raiding parties. King Edward I (The Hammer of the Scots) died here on July 7th 1307, and his body was laid out in the village. The church is built on the site of the Roman Fort – Aballva. Out in the marshes you will find a sandstone monument erected in his honour, at the place he died whilst waiting to cross the river to subdue Robert the Bruce, King of Scotland. His long campaign resulted in considerable destruction and death in the Lake District and as a consequence local communities, determined to resist further massacre, built defensive structures known as Pele Towers. These included massive church towers here and at St Michaels at Bowness, which also doubled up as bell towers.

 ## ACCOMMODATION

Hillside Farm, Boustead Hill, Burgh by Sands, Carlisle CA5 6AA

Run by: Sandra Rudd

Ideal for groups, this charming Georgian Grade II listed farmhouse has a splendid bunkhouse in a splendidly converted stable. Stunning views across the marshes and sands to Scotland. You can leave your car here and there's a secure lock-up. The bunkhouse sleeping area now separate from living area.

Rooms: 1D/T, 1T.
B&B: £27 (£30 single occ).
Bunkhouse: sleeps 13, £10 a night.
Breakfast from £4.
Cooking facilities and pots/pans provided.
Drying facilities VisitBritain: 3-stars.
Graded bunkhouse.
01228 576398
ruddshillside1@btinternet.com
hadrianswalkbnb.co.uk

ROUTE DESCRIPTION

You continue along the line of the Roman Road to Drumburgh. The remains of the railway runs on your left and the wall, which was probably built of earth in this area, is over across the marshes on the right. When the new town of Silloth was created in 1854, with a deepwater dock into the Solway, the railway was again modified with a new line from Drumburgh through to Silloth. Then the construction of the Bowness-on-Solway Railway Viaduct so altered the deepwater channels that Port Carlisle silted up and was abandoned. The branch line though was maintained as a Victorian tourist route with horse drawn Dandy carriages from Drumburgh.

ACCOMMODATION

Hope & Anchor, Port Carlisle, Wigton, Cumbria CA7 5BU
Run by: Joe Hancock & Jonathan Breeze
Cracking home cooked food and three real ales, mostly from a 20-mile radius. This is a lovely and isolated spot on a beautiful stretch of the Solway Firth. Recently and stylishly renovated the Hope is a beacon of homely comfort in one of the remotest and loveliest stretches of the ride. There's a secure lock-up and a boiler room for drying out kit. Part of the Cyclists Welcome scheme. Very obliging and right on the route. Look out for interesting items on the specials board. Open all day. Dogs welcome, no charge.
Rooms: 1D, 1T, 1F (1D & 2S)
B&B: £35 (no single supp).
Discounts for children.
Eve meal: from £6.75.
Pk lunch: Yes. Flexible on this.
Pse pre-order. VisitBritain: 4 stars
016973 51460
mrjonathanhiggins@yahoo.co.uk
hopeandanchorinn.com

BOWNESS-ON-SOLWAY

Bowness-on-Solway was the end of the Wall and the most northern frontier of the Roman Empire after its withdrawal from the Antonine Wall between Edinburgh and Glasgow. The Bowness Roman fort of Maia was the second largest fort on Hadrian's Wall and the village is largely built upon its site. St Michael's Church is built over its granary. All the way along this coast there are sands and marshes and views across to Scotland well worth lingering over.

About half a mile on you pass the remains of the Solway viaduct, over a mile long, which crossed the river to Annan. The Solway Viaduct spanned 2544 yards and provided a direct route to Glasgow from the ore fields of West Cumbria and bypassed the congestion at Carlisle where seven railway companies, with seven engine sheds and depots, all jostled for space. The viaduct was repeatedly damaged by winter ice and was finally demolished in 1934. Local lore suggests that one reason for its closure was that the Scots, who at that time had no access to alcohol on Sundays, used to walk across to Bowness and occasionally fell off and drowned on their return trip.

▶ ROUTE DESCRIPTION

Hadrian's Cycleway now follows the coast but you can take alternative short cut routes across to Whitrigg and Angerton. Newton Arlosh was created in the early 1300s to replace the village of Skinburness where the monks of Holme Cultrum Abbey panned for salt. This continued until the 1690s. If you visit the church of St John's note that the door is only 2 feet 7 inches high as it was built with defence in mind against the Border Reivers who were active at the time. It was said that at weddings the first of the bridal pair out of the church would be the boss.

Seaville was the home of the late John Naylor who constructed all the railway paths you will meet through Workington and Whitehaven. Whilst he was alive Sustrans had ambitions to construct a new route through the marshes to reach Skinburness and you might still like to take the main road through Calvo to pick up the Sea Dyke road to Skinburness for the full coastal experience. If you have time walk out to Grune Point which is a noted spot for bird watching, particularly at high tides. If you are interested in war time defences, the Cumberland Machine Gun and Anti Tank Rifle Emplacement is a design of pill box unique to West Cumberland, whilst the Skinburness Mile fortlet formed part of the so called western sea defences, an extension of Hadrian's work which stretched from Bowness-on-Solway all the way down to Ravenglass.

Bowness-on-Solwa

Silloth

Abbeytown

Allonby

Maryport

A596

Flimby

A595

Workington

A66

Cockermouth

SILLOTH → WORKINGTON

SILLOTH

22 miles (mostly on-road)

Silloth was a planned town built in the 1850s around the new deepwater port. You will notice the wide tree-lined streets and the extensive sea front green, with magnificent promenade stretching back to Skinburness. Don't rush through Silloth. It has a memorable end of the road and edge of the land feel, and it's certainly not on the road to anywhere, so it might be a while before you come again. Its name derives from the 'Lathes' or barns which were used to store grain and were located close to the sea, thus 'sea lathes'. The great English singer Kathleen Ferrier, for whom Benjamin Britten wrote several works, moved to Silloth back in 1936, when the town was booming.

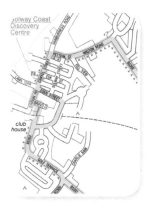

🔭 PLACES OF INTEREST

Tourist Information Centre,
Solway Coast Discovery Centre (see below).

Solway Coast Discovery Centre, Liddell St, CA7 4DD (016973 31944). Film tour – shows coastal highlights. There are also frequent temporary exhibitions. 2006 marked the 40th anniversary of the Solway Coast being designated an AONB (Area of Outstanding Natural Beauty) and the Discovery Centre helps bring this to life with a fascinating montage of how the area developed from the Ice Age through to modern times. Lots of interesting facts about the Viking settlements here and the plethora of Viking place names.

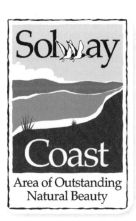

231

For further information on the area, contact **The Solway Coast AONB Management**, Liddell St, Silloth, CA7 4DD. 016973 31944, solwaycoastaonb.org.uk

The Solway Coast AONB was designated in 1964 and covers 44 square miles (115 sq km) of the Cumbrian coastline between Rockcliffe and Maryport. It is one of 37 AONBs in England, which, like the National Parks, are protected as our finest landscapes.

Find out more about cycling in Cumbria:
cyclingcumbria.co.uk

Should you wish to spend more time exploring the Solway coast, take a look at the website hadrian-guide.co.uk for five wonderful cycle loops.

 WHERE TO EAT

CUPS & SAUCERS FARM TEA SHOP, Seaville Farm, Silloth, CA7 4PT Run by: Kathleen Hughes. Good spot to stop for a well-earned break. Open fire and even a hot tub. Mid-way between Abbey Town and Silloth. 01697 361256 | croftlandscourt.co.uk.

THE GINCASE, with its Farmhouse Tearoom, is an ideal stop-off, with a fine range of home baking and local produce. Serves morning coffee, lunch and afternoon tea which – weather permitting – you can enjoy in the orchard. There's a Craft Barn and a Gallery of local art, plus a farm park for the kids. The Gincase, Mawbray Hayrigg, Silloth, CA7 4LL. 016973 32020 | gincase.co.uk.

BANK MILL NURSERIES, Beckfoot, Silloth, CA7 4LF. It is on the B5300 just north of Mawbray and has a coffee shop, which does coffees, homemade soups, paninis and big breakfast baguettes, cakes and pastries, scones and sinful rum butter. There's also a fully licensed bistro open daily (except Mon & Tues) between 1800-2200 (last order 2100). There's a butterfly house and nature reserve. 01900 881340 | bankmillnurseries.co.uk

▶ ROUTE INFORMATION

From now on the route diverts inland in order to avoid at least some of the rather fast coastal road, which we rejoin just north of Allonby. Intead of heading right onto the B5300 you carry straight on to the crossroads at Balladoyle, where you head right, passing The Gincase. If you do opt to take the B5300, take great care as it is a fast and narrow road with little or no verge. There are plans to have a cycle track and our Cycle Guides website hadrian-route.co.uk will let you know when this project comes to fruition.

ALLONBY

Allonby, among other things, boasts an exceptional ice cream shop. Once an important centre for herring fishing, in Victorian times Allonby became a coastal resort. Despite its modest size the village has several splendid buildings. Alfred Waterhouse, who also designed Manchester's Town Hall and the Natural History Museum in London, designed the Reading Room. Charles Dickens and Wilkie Collins are both reputed to have stayed at The Ship Inn whilst JMW Turner painted the sunsets from Silloth. In the 18th century this remote shoreline became a favourite  place for landing contraband stored on the tax free haven of the Isle of Man.

Near Allonby is Beckfoot (known as Bibra by the Romans). Coastal erosion here – hard by the B5300 – has exposed a Roman cemetery where urns and other artifacts are being rescued by English Heritage.

▶ ROUTE INFORMATION

At Bank End do stop off at the fortlet which has been excavated and gives you some idea of what this part of the Roman defence system looked like. It is also an excellent place to photograph the rest of your party cycling away down the coastal road.

At Bank End turn off the road through the golf club, who are very welcoming with refreshments, and join the promenade to Maryport. This point marks the start of long lengths of traffic-free path. High on the hill above the promenade is Senhouse Roman Museum which can be reached by peeling off on one of the narrow tarmac paths leading to the Roman fort. Maryport was the command and supply base for the coastal defences of Hadrian's Wall and was occupied for nearly 300 years. The town was developed by Humphrey Senhouse in 1756, who called the town Maryport after his wife Mary. The Maryport and Carlisle railway opened in 1845 and the docks flourished, exporting rails and cast iron. They were the largest docks on the West Cumbrian coast until 1927, when Barrow was built.

MARYPORT

Maryport is a good place to stop, with an attractive centre, revived docks and new arts centre.

📷 PLACES OF INTEREST

Maryport Tourist Information Centre
Town Hall, Senhouse Street
01900 812101

The Wave, Irish Street, 01900 811450
The Wave is an imaginative and airy £3.3million Entertainment, Conferencing and Heritage Visitor Centre in the historic Georgian harbour of Maryport.

THE COMPLEX FEATURES

Theatre, Concert Hall and Conference Centre

Interactive Heritage Visitor Centre

Bar and Café/Bistro

Gift Shop featuring 'Made In Cumbria' Arts and Crafts

Tourist Information Centre

Theatre & Cinema

The Main Theatre is a multi-functional space that will feature professional theatre and music performances, cinema, local community arts performances. There's seating for 234.

Heritage Visitor Centre
The Heritage Visitor Centre features interactive displays journeying through Maryport's past and promoting attractions in the town and areas of special interest. Learn about Ship Building in the town and Maryport's links with the Titanic.

Tourist Information Centre
The Centre also houses Maryport's Tourist Information Centre providing information on events, attractions and an on line accommodation booking system. So whatever it is you need to know – just ask.
thewavemaryport.co.uk

The Wave Café/Bistro
Offers light snacks, lunches, refreshments and a bistro menu in an agreeably light modern eating area. All food is fresh and homemade on the premises. There is a fully stocked licensed bar and a catering service for special events. There's also a gift shop which stocks handcrafted gifts and artwork supplied by Made In Cumbria, as well as an extensive range of books.

Lake District Coast Aquarium
The award winning Lake District Coast Aquarium, specialising in native British aquatic life, has some fantastic displays of our weird and wonderful fishy neighbours.
01900 817760
coastaquarium.co.uk

Maritime Museum
Shipping Brow
Tells the story of the docks, the town and Maryport's most famous inhabitants, such as Henry Ismay, founder of the White Star Line (of Titanic fame) and the family of Fletcher Christian, of the Mutiny on the Bounty.
01900 813738

Maryport Golf Club
Bank End, Maryport, Cumbria
Situated on the Solway Firth. Maryport golf club represents a unique golfing experience in Cumbria. You can enjoy a round of golf that is part traditional links and part parkland, whilst enjoying views of Criffel and South Scotland.
maryportgolfclub.co.uk

Senhouse Roman Museum
Housed in a Victorian Naval Reserve Battery this award winning museum houses the largest collection of Roman altars from a single site in Britain and lies adjacent to the clifftop fort of Alauna, part of the Hadrian's Wall World Heritage Site.
01900 816168.
senhousemuseum.co.uk

The Harbour Lights Project
Maryport Harbour
The Harbour lights project is a series of permanent contemporary art installations set in and around the historic harbour.

CAPTAIN NELSON, Irish Street, Maryport
open: Daily 11.30 am - 2pm including bank Holidays
01900 813109

CROSS QUAYS FISH 'N' CHIPS, 15 King Street, Maryport,
01900 815956

CURZON GRILL, Curzon Street, Maryport
Open: Mon-Thurs 8.30am –9.30pm Fri & Sat 8.30am-10pm Sun
10am-9pm Also Bank Holidays, 01900 819265

EMPIRE COFFEE SHOP & SANDWICH BAR, Senhouse Street,
Maryport. open: Mon-Sat 9am-5pm Wed 9am-4pm.
01900 817760

HONG KONG (Chinese)
119 Crosby Street, Maryport
01900 812007

MCMENAMINS, Irish Street, Maryport
01900 819777, mcmenamins.co.uk

PEARL GARDEN CANTONESE CUISINE, 44 Wood Street,
Maryport 01900 818888

PEDRO'S, 92 Senhouse Street, Maryport, 01900 816624

PORT OF CALL, Senhouse Street
open: Daily including Bank Holidays, 01900 810128

THE LAKE DISTRICT COAST AQUARIUM, South Quay, Maryport. Open: Daily including Bank Holidays. Closed Christmas Day
& Boxing Day
01900 817760, lakedistrict-coastaquarium.co.uk

THE LIFEBOAT INN & HARBOUR RESTAURANT
Shipping Brow, Senhouse Street, Maryport, Cumbria
open: Restaurant 7pm-9.30
0190010906,

THE WAVE, Irish Street, Maryport
open: Daily, 01900 811450, thewavemaryport.co.uk

THE WAVERLEY HOTEL AND LA SCALZI (Italian) Resturant
Curzon Street, Maryport. Open: Mon - Sat 12pm - 2pm &
6.30pm - 9pm, Sun 12pm - 2pm & 7pm - 9pm (La Scalzi Closed
Monday only), 01900 812115

Route information and background

South of Maryport you will be following a purpose built cycle route nearly all the way to Seascale, south of Sellafield. This has been something of an heroic adventure occupying Sustrans, Groundwork and the Councils for the best part of the last 20 years. One recent addition is the new path south of the docks, past the reclaimed waste heaps to pass under the railway and on to Flimby. Ideas for a coastal route following the narrow strip of dunes between station and sea proved too difficult and you now follow an inland track to St Helens, and then a new roadside path past the Oldside and Siddick line of windmills on your right and the paperworks on your left, to join the start of a long series of railway paths.

The railway routes we follow are just some of the lines built in West Cumbria during a few frantic years in the mid 19th century. Coal was mined and exported by sea from 1650 onwards from Workington, Parton and Whitehaven, and early on horse drawn waggonways were made with at least eight lines in the Whitehaven area by 1820. We follow the one at Parton. The first railway here was the Maryport and Carlisle, built in 1845 by George Stephenson, and by 1850 the coastal line was open all the way to Furness. This all remains as the current mainline railway.

The route follows the lines built to serve the burgeoning steelworks. The Whitehaven, Clearwater and Egremont opened in 1866 and the diversionary line 'Way of the Ironmasters', built to avoid the punitive LNWR charges on the coastal route, opened from Siddick in 1879. But by 1880 the industry was already on the wane, the fabulous haematite mines worked out and the Ironmasters were importing Spanish ores. Gradually the mines closed – the last was an ore mine at Beckermet in 1982, and the last coal mine, Haig Pit at Whitehaven, in 1986. By then most of the inland railways were closed. This decline was the cyclist's good fortune and some 30 miles are incorporated into Sustrans C2C Routes, which themselves then became a catalyst for the whole National Cycle Network. As you cycle along these green and tranquil paths it is difficult to imagine the industry of every description which worked here scarcely 100 years ago, and all the more incongruous because of the area's association with the Lake District.

WORKINGTON

Starting at Siddick on the 'Way of the Ironmasters', the land was all reclaimed from the sea. The lake on your left was original sea marsh. Beyond the lake above the sea cliff runs the railway path to Seaton and Cockermouth, part of the C2C route, covering the site of the Burgh Walls coastal fort now buried by the railway embankment. In the early stages of planning this cycle route Sustrans proposed the construction of a replica catapult to fire Hillman Imps over the lake to crash in a heap of ruined cars on the lower railway! The hills on the right, the seaward side, are in fact slag heaps and if you come across Jem Southam's recent photographic exhibition you will see how extraordinary this artificial coastline is. Just south of the junction between the two railway paths the route curls backward and forwards in a landscape sculpture designed by Mark Merror to create a point of interest in this derelict cutting. As you cross the River Derwent you will see a branch running along the river. This was opened to Cockermouth (1847), and if you follow this you will come to the lighthouse which forms the start of this branch of the C2C, with its panoramic view of the Lakes.

A potted history

Once the centre of the steelmaking industry, Henry Bessemer developed his revolutionary blast furnace here in 1857; at one stage its rolling mills produced rails for railways in almost every country in the world. By 1909 all the local works – Maryport, Oldside, Derwent, Moss Bay and Harrington – had merged into the Workington Iron and Steel Co. and after a final hectic period through the Great War the industry was worked out. From 1930 a single integrated 'Combine' survived at Workington, but the last Bessemer 'blow' was in 1975, the blast furnace shut down in 1982, and the rolling mills in 2007, when the work was transferred to Scunthorpe.

If you have time to wander down to the coast you will walk below a wholly man-made cliffscape, where the sea beats against slag and the detritus from making rails sent all over the world from Bolivia to India, and from Scotland to Capetown. Echoes from the steel heart of Britain's industrial zenith.

Images of the Solway Coastline: 'Area of Outstanding Beauty.'

Accommodation

✱ ← For full details see page 42

Morven House Hotel, Siddick Rd, Workington, Cumbria CA14 1LE
01900 602118, morvenguesthouse.com
cnelsonmorven@aol.com

Armidale Cottages, 29 High Seaton, CA14 1PD
01900 63704, armidalecottages.co.uk
armidalecotts@hotmail.com

Waverley Hotel
01900 65892, waverley-hotel.com
waverley-hotel@btconnect.com

▶ ROUTE DESCRIPTION

● In Workington itself the route runs through a car park on the old station site, which makes a convenient stopping point for shopping, before continuing to Distington. Here the once tranquil railway path has been blighted by the new A595 trunk road and the route that you follow is the result of long and not wholly satisfactory battles with the Highways Agency.

● You pass briefly through Lowca where coal was mined for centuries, locomotives were manufactured and a chemical works set up to develop coal by-products in 1911. This was famous for being shelled by German submarines in 1915. You rejoin the coast at Parton, below yet another Roman fortlet. It is worth stopping here to reflect that this minute cluster of buildings started life as an anchorage used by the Romans. By Elizabethan times small merchant vessels were trading from here carrying Moresby's coal to Chester. A cluster of industries developed in this little valley including saltpans, glassworks, the Lowca Engineering Company, which made the first locomotive for the Maryport and Carlisle Railway, which had to be shipped north by barge. There was also a large tannery squeezed in, but soon the whole area was taken over by a colliery which mined through the Parton Drift Tunnel, carrying the coal away by horse drawn waggonway to Whitehaven Port.

● We follow this tramway for a quite magnificent section of the ride with views north on a clear day to the Galloway Coast, above the mainline railway cut into the cliff below, right above the sea.

WORKINGTON → RAVENGLASS

32 miles (mostly on-road)

WHITEHAVEN

Whitehaven is a highlight and is discussed elsewhere as the start of the C2C. Don't rush through, but enjoy the Georgian planned town, with its redeveloped harbour, the Beacon Visitor Centre, and the Haig Colliery Mining Museum high on the cliffs above the town.

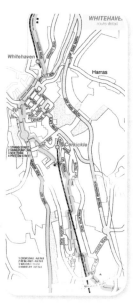

From Whitehaven to Moor Row Hadrian's Cycleway follows the line of the original C2C route opened in 1994. Notice the two seats constructed from bridge beams. The first of these is positioned exactly on the line of the railway with the beams 4 foot 8 and a half inches apart where they hit the ground to reflect the original gauge of the railways. The path diverts around the seats with the result that you get a wonderful view looking up the railway.

To mark each mile large rocks were brought in at the time of construction and positioned to reflect local history or interest. This route was built by Sustrans and Groundwork in 1991 and 1992 and considerable effort was placed on drawing in the local communities along the route by means of public art and other items of interest.

You will pass a number of steel way markers, all created by local schools under the guidance of Richard Farrington. At Moor Row the signpost consists simply of a whole school class's names, but all to the same purpose of giving character to the route and ownership to locals to win their support and care for it. Just before passing under the main road bridge you can divert away onto the minor road to St Bees (for accommodation in St Bees (see below) which is the start of Wainwright's Walk and would have also been a start of the C2C route had it been possible to construct a new path parallel to the railway to avoid this hilly road.

Just beyond Moor Row the route splits in all directions. Go to the left and you soon come to the Lady Victoria Mine which reputedly took coal, iron and limestone from the same shaft and now is surmounted by the Rock Crusher sculpture. Go straight on and you are on the way to Consett and Sunderland. Continue right along our route on the line of the Whitehaven, Cleator and Egremont Railway, and you pass a number of interesting bridges.

First under the path runs a pedestrian tunnel where you walk on steel plates under which the Beck runs – a double deck bridge! You then cross over an old footbridge relocated from Egremont station and then under an elegant elliptical arch before rejoining the road. On the way you cross Wainwright's Coast to Coast Walk from St Bees to Robin Hoods Bay. Stop here at the junction to Cleator Village to take in the vista of the Lakeland hills and Dent Fell laid out before you.

 ## ACCOMMODATION

✳ ◆ For full details see page 30-31

Chestnuts, Low Moresby, Whitehaven, Cumbria, CA28 6RX
01946 61612, owlmagic@tesco.net
chestnuts-whitehaven.com

Glenard Guest House, Inkerman Terr, Whitehaven, CA28 7TY
01946 692249, info@glenard.co.uk
glenard.co.uk

Chase Hotel, Inkerman Terrace, Whitehaven CA28 8AA
01946 693656 | chase1@tms-connect.co.uk
chasewhitehaven.co.uk

Moresby Hall, Moresby, Whitehaven, Cumbria, CA28 6PJ
01946 696317, info@moresbyhall.co.uk
moresbyhall.co.uk

Glenfield House, Corkickle, CA28 7TS
01946 691911, glenfieldhousewhitehaven@gmail.com
glenfieldhousewhitehaven.co.uk

Summergrove Halls, Hensingham, Whitehaven Cumbria CA28 8XZ
01946 813328, info@summergrovehalls.co.uk
summergrovehalls.co.uk

ST BEES

St Bees enjoys all the benefits of the Lake District without the dense throngs. Most of the time. That's one of the advantages to being off the beaten track. It is famously the start of the Coast to Coast walk, mapped and then popularised by Alfred Wainright nearly 40 years ago. Its gentle sandy coastal setting, framed by thrusting cliffs, separates it starkly from the Workington and Whitehaven alternative start points, and its popularity with cyclists grows year on year.

It is best known for St Bees School, a 400 year old public school and the Priory of St Mary and St Bega, which dates back to 1120. St Bees Head is its most pronounced feature, the most westerly point in northern England. Remarkably, this is the only major sea cliff between Wales and Scotland, and seethes with so much birdlife that it is a Site of Special Scientific Interest.

Its theological college, now gone, was set up in 1816 and was the only one outside Oxford and Cambridge. There could be few more tranquil places for contemplation.

There is plenty of accommodation here as well as a rail link.

Queens Hotel, Main St, St Bees, Cumbria, CA27 0DE

Run by: Mark Smedley

The project to completely refurbish this 17th century inn is now complete. The Queen's has a cosy country pub atmosphere, with oak beams and log fires. There are two real ale bars and a decent wine list. The restaurant has been stylishly redesigned and all meals are cooked on the premises using locally sourced ingredients where possible. Large conservatory and terraced garden. Secure cycle storage.

Rooms: 3S, 4T, 1F, 5D.
B&B: £27-£47.
Eve meal: from £6.95.
Pk lunch: from £4.95.
01946 822287
enquiries@queenshotelstbees.co.uk
queenshotelstbees.co.uk

Fairladies Barn Guest House, Main St, St Bees, Cumbria CA27 0AD

Run by: Will & Nicola Corrie

Luxury accommodation at affordable prices in an attractive converted 17th century sandstone barn, which stands back from the upper end of the high street, with a sun trap garden area. Fairladies looks as if it has been transported from one of those picture postcard villages in the Dordogne.

Rooms: 4D, 3T, 2F
(1D & 1T with shared bathroom).
B&B: £32.50. £45 single.
Eve meal: Lots of nearby pubs.
Pk lunch: £6.
01946 822718
info@fairladiesbarn.co.uk
fairladiesbarn.co.uk

▶ ROUTE DESCRIPTION

Now on to Thornhill, beside the trunk road, for a short section of railway path which slots through a gap in the houses and beside a garage yard, for minor roads to Beckermet – at the meeting of Black Beck and Kirk Beck.

Seascale

Go straight if you want to get some idea of the size of the Sellafield operation. Sadly they have closed their visitor centre. Or go right to pick up the final section along the diversionary railway and the coast again at Sellafield marshalling yards and pick up the path through the dunes to Seascale.

This last traffic-free section is particularly magnificent, confined as it is between the railway and the sea. Here Sustrans have introduced a variety of techniques to produce a narrow path which gives a memorable ride through the shifting sands. Seascale is another coastal resort which flourished as a result of the Victorian Furness Railway (1850). The beach is magnificent and empty, and at some states of the tide is firm enough to cycle on if you are so inclined.

Accommodation

Calder House Hotel, The Banks, Seascale, CA20 1QP.
Run by: Andy Gainford & Steve Ainley
An imposing Victorian former girls' boarding school, perched above the sands seven miles from Ravenglass. Calder House is now a charming, old-fashioned, well-run seaside hotel with good beers, well priced and well chosen wines, and a competitive and inviting menu. Great value and a real throw back to the Edwardian era.
Rooms: 4T, 12D.
B&B: £30-£40.
Secure lock up.
019467 28538
info@calderhouse.co.uk
calderhouse.co.uk

Shepherds Views Campsite

Run by: Julie & Stephen Shepherd

Attractive campsite and cottages for rent close to the route between Ravenglass and Seascale, 5 miles from start/end of route so is an ideal last night or first night place to pitch your tent, with stunning views across the National Park. Set in 210 acres of farmland, there's plenty of space for caravans, too. Underfloor heating at the family amenity block and plenty of showers. Secure cycle lock-up plus hose-down facilities. Also cottages for rent for those wanting to stay for a few days and explore.

70 licensed plots. £10.50 per pitch (high season)
£8.50 low season.
£3 per adult.
3 cottages for rent.
019467 29907
contact@shepherdsviews.co.uk
shepherdsviews.co.uk

GOSFORTH

The long awaited cyclepath from Seascale to Gosforth is almost complete, Route 727, linking the vibrant and scenic village to Hadrian's Cycleway. It is just over two miles along the B5344 to get to Gosforth, but the road is far from ideal, so be warned. Gosforth has much needed accommodation and a couple of excellent places to eat, so provides an ideal alternative to Ravenglass for a last or first night stopover.

On the edge of the Western Lakes, set within the Cumbrian National Park and close to the Wasdale and Eskdale valleys (not to mention the beautiful coastline). The village is a popular destination for those wishing to explore this quiet corner of the lakes.